Oyster Worldwide

Hodore Farm, Hartfield
East Sussex, TN7 4AR
United Kingdom
t: +44 (0) 1892 770 771
www.oysterworldwide.com

BEAR
sanctuary

VICTOR WATKINS

This book is dedicated to my father
who encouraged me to write.

Contents

Plan of the Romanian bear sanctuary.

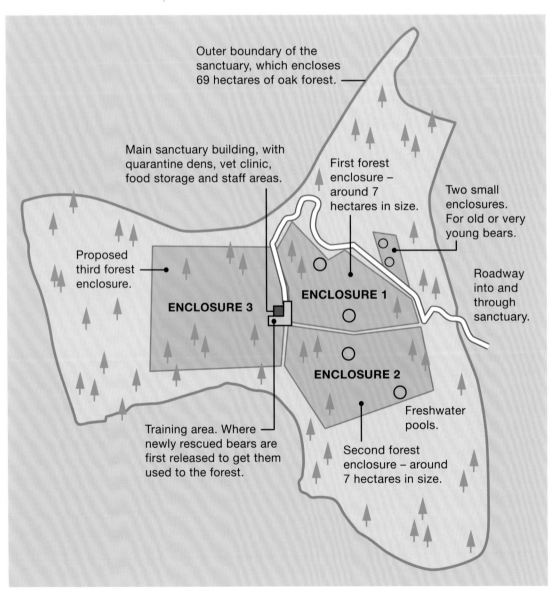

Outer boundary of the sanctuary, which encloses 69 hectares of oak forest.

Main sanctuary building, with quarantine dens, vet clinic, food storage and staff areas.

First forest enclosure – around 7 hectares in size.

Two small enclosures. For old or very young bears.

Proposed third forest enclosure.

Roadway into and through sanctuary.

ENCLOSURE 1

ENCLOSURE 3

ENCLOSURE 2

Freshwater pools.

Training area. Where newly rescued bears are first released to get them used to the forest.

Second forest enclosure – around 7 hectares in size.

About the author

Victor Watkins has worked in the field of international animal welfare for the past 30 years undertaking investigations into a variety of issues including the farming of bears for their bile, the trade in dogs for human consumption, bullfighting, fur farming, and the illegal traffic in wildlife.

In 1991 he set up the world's first international campaign to protect bears from cruelty in the wild and in captivity. This campaign, called Libearty, was run by the World Society for the Protection of Animals (WSPA) for whom Victor is a Wildlife Advisor.

Over the past two decades Victor has worked with animal groups around the world to highlight the exploitation of bears and to gain public and government support to end cruel practices such as dancing bears in Europe and Asia, bear farming in Asia, bear-baiting in Pakistan and the use of captive bears for public entertainment.

Victor initiated the concept of the bear sanctuary in 1992 to enable the Greek and Turkish governments to eradicate the use of dancing bears in their countries. All the dancing bears were confiscated and placed in purpose-built forest sanctuaries in those countries.

Since then bear sanctuaries have been built in countries such as Bulgaria, Thailand, Pakistan, China, Vietnam and North America to allow for the rescue of bears from illegal or poor captive conditions. The most recent bear sanctuary is in central Romania and is known

as the Libearty Bear Sanctuary. At the time of publication of this book it was caring for 56 rescued bears.

Victor has been involved in the making of a number of TV documentaries on wildlife protection, the latest being a series of programmes featuring the Romanian bear sanctuary on the Animal Planet TV channel.

Victor hopes that this book will encourage a wider appreciation of the need to protect bears from exploitation. He hopes that more governments and organisations will try to protect these magnificent wild animals in their natural habitats.

Introduction

TO MOST PEOPLE OUTSIDE OF ROMANIA, THE name Transylvania conjures up an immediate image of Count Dracula and vampires, as immortalised in so many films, TV documentaries and of course the original book written by Bram Stoker back in 1897. But to those living in the heart of Transylvania itself, the creatures that most often spring to mind are less bat shaped and more bear shaped.

Around 6,000 European brown bears inhabit the Carpathian Mountains which curl majestically through the Romanian countryside, more bears than can be found in any other European country today. Romania has been one of the last remaining strongholds for European brown bears, but their forest habitat is now under increasing threat from expanding industrialisation and agriculture which is reaching into the forests and mountains of this once tranquil and rural area of Europe.

When bears live in forests near to human habitation there is inevitably going to be some form of conflict as the bears seek out better and easier food sources in the agricultural crops, beehives, grazing livestock and also the rubbish bins that are located near to the forests.

When bears are seen as a threat to people, the usual solution is to hunt them. Many human-bear conflicts are the result of mother bears seeking out extra food for their cubs. Killing the mother bears leaves orphaned bear cubs which may then be caught by the hunters.

A very young bear cub has sufficient 'teddy bear' appeal to ensure that captured cubs often end up in cages as pets, but cute cubs grow into strong animals in the space of six months and these caged animals soon become neglected curiosities.

That is where the story of the Romanian bear sanctuary begins. Bears thrived in the wild in Romania in the 1970s and 80s because of the protection given to them by the Romanian Dictator Nicolae Ceausescu. He banned hunting for everyone except himself and those close to him, but when hunting resumed after the dictator's death in 1990, many young bears ended up in captivity and languished in poorly constructed cages with inadequate diets.

By the dawning of the 21st century there had already been a decade of growing public and legislative support around the world against the keeping of bears in poor captive conditions. Sanctuaries for rescued bears were being created in countries such as Greece, Turkey, India and even China. The once-captive bears could no longer fend for themselves if released to the wild so the alternative was to provide them with a smaller, safer, protected forest sanctuary for life.

These bear sanctuaries were mostly areas of natural forest surrounded by protective fences to keep the bears in and people out. This meant that bears could be rescued from poor and often illegal captive conditions and released into large areas with trees, earth, grass and fresh water pools where they would spend the rest of their lives.

As Romania edged towards membership of the European Union, with the new laws that this would demand, the time was ripe for the country to reassess its treatment of captive wild animals.

In 2005 work began on the creation of the Romanian bear sanctuary – a large forest area protected by perimeter fences which would be home for brown bears rescued from their cramped cages around the country. It would provide trees, fresh water pools, hibernation dens and large areas of meadow and forest where the once-captive bears would be able to taste the freedom of nature for the first time in their lives since they were captured from the wild as cubs.

The sanctuary would enable the Romanian authorities to enforce laws against keeping bears in poor captive conditions, and would see an end to the illegal capture of bear cubs from the wild and their use as tourist attractions in front of restaurants and ski resorts.

The sanctuary was built in the oak forests above the town of Zarnesti in Transylvania through the determination of people such as Cristina and Roger Lapis and with the support of an international animal welfare organisation, the World Society for the Protection of Animals (WSPA), who believed the sanctuary needed to be built. They achieved what many people said would be an impossible task.

Now the children of Romania can visit the sanctuary and watch these bears playing in the water pools or sunbathing in the meadows. They can learn why their native wildlife is so precious and how their bears and other wild animals should be protected in their natural habitats for future generations to enjoy.

Bear Sanctuary is the story of the plight of both captive and wild bears in Romania and how there is hope for the future of these majestic animals to live in peace in the forests of the Carpathian Mountains.

What is a bear sanctuary?

THE ORIGINAL CONCEPT AND DESIGN OF THE bear sanctuary was created by the World Society for the Protection of Animals (WSPA) in the early 1990s to enable the eradication of the cruel trade in dancing bears in Greece and Turkey. All the dancing bears were legally confiscated and given their freedom in the bear sanctuaries, designed and built by the WSPA with support from local animal groups and government departments in those countries. Since then many more sanctuaries for rescued bears have been developed around the world by the WSPA and by other organisations.

Bear sanctuaries were created to enable bears to be rescued from a poor life in captivity. A 'Sanctuary' is a place of shelter and protection and the aim of a bear sanctuary is to provide the rescued animals with an environment that allows them to exhibit such natural behaviours as foraging for food, swimming, climbing and even hibernation. In the majority of cases the rescued bears are old, have teeth, claw or eyesight problems, and have been in captivity too long to consider trying to release them back to the wild as they simply would not survive. The sanctuary is therefore like a retirement home for them.

A bear sanctuary should ideally be an area of forest situated within natural bear habitat, surrounded by a protective fence to keep the rescued animals in and to keep people and other wild animals out.

The perimeter fence can be made of weldmesh fencing or stone walls (2 to 3 metres high) which provide an important visual barrier. But the main protective barrier is a series of electric wires running along the inside of the fence or wall from ground level to the top, carrying a charge of around 7,000 volts. Bears usually approach the fence with their nose and the shock they receive from touching the wires does not injure them but is sharp enough to prevent the animals from attempting to climb the fence or wall. The fence (or wall) foundations extend up to 1.5 metres into the ground to prevent the animals from digging underneath.

The bear sanctuaries built by the WSPA consist of one or more forested enclosures with accompanying buildings for staff and veterinary care. Quarantine den areas are used for newly rescued bears so they can acclimatise before being released into the forest. A forest enclosure of around 6 hectares (15 acres), the size of 6 international rugby fields, is sufficient to house 30 or more bears. Each enclosure should have several fresh water pools, plenty of trees to climb, and dens or shaded areas in which to sleep, hibernate or to escape from the weather.

Although the bears can forage for plants and other natural food sources in the forest enclosure, their diet has to be supplemented by a regular supply of food provided by the sanctuary staff. Fruit and vegetables, bread and even honey are some of the foods given to the

sanctuary bears as an addition to the plants, roots, berries and nuts found growing within the forest enclosures. Food storage and preparation areas built into the sanctuary buildings ensure that fruit and vegetables can be kept in cold storage until needed.

Trained support staff deal with all aspects of the initial rescue and subsequent daily feeding and care of the bears, as well as the maintenance of the sanctuary enclosure and facilities.

above: A bear's natural forest habitat.
below: A well-deserved rest after a day's foraging.

Veterinary inspections and treatment of newly rescued animals can be performed in the on-site veterinary clinic.

The rescued bears go through a quarantine procedure where they are given thorough veterinary checks and surgical operations are performed if required. Some may need teeth or eye treatment and all bears need an improved diet to bring them back to good health.

When they are healthy enough, they are released into the main forest enclosure where they can mix with other bears and integrate fully into life in the sanctuary.

Rescued bears are prevented from breeding by undergoing sterilisation. Breeding would increase the pressure on the numbers of animals in the sanctuary, so all adult male bears brought to the sanctuary are surgically castrated. However, if there is the possibility of some of the younger animals being released back into the wild at some stage, these animals should not be sterilised.

opposite and right: Bears enjoying the freedom of the bear sanctuary.

Where possible the sanctuary should also be used as an educational centre where the public, especially school children, can have restricted viewing of the animals and can learn not only why the animals were brought to the sanctuary, but also about bears and the need to protect them in the wild.

It has to be ensured that public viewing does not compromise the welfare of the animals. The bears are free to hide away in the forest or wander in the meadows in full view of the public. Visitors can view the animals from a distance but should not be able to interact, feed or otherwise affect the animals' behaviour. Most bears brought to a sanctuary have previously been in some form of captive situation and have had contact with people, so in a sanctuary they are likely to be unconcerned about the proximity of people the other side of the fence. In fact they quickly get used to the sanctuary staff who feed them daily by scattering food over the perimeter fence.

There is a clear distinction between this type of bear sanctuary and a zoo. It may be said that if the public are allowed to view the bears in a sanctuary, it is similar to a zoo, but the big difference between these two facilities is in the welfare of the bears.

Many zoos around the world keep bears and other animals in small enclosures, usually with concrete floors, cage bars and a small water trough. Of course there are better zoos which try to provide a larger area with some natural vegetation, but in general the zoo animals are always on show for the public. They have no place to hide away from the gaze of the visitors, and in most cases they are unable to exhibit their natural behaviour such as digging, climbing and swimming. Many zoos also tend to breed bears and other animals for their displays or to sell on to other zoos.

Bears in the sanctuaries have been legally rescued from poor captive conditions, do not breed, and are free to move into the deep forest or out into the exposed meadows as they wish. The bears are not there for the entertainment of visitors and the visiting public have to be aware that they may not even see any bears if the animals prefer to rest out of sight in the forest. They are basically retirement homes for rescued animals.

The educational value of showing people, especially children, bears digging in the earth, climbing trees and being relaxed enough to play-fight with each other gives people a far better impression of what these animals are really like than if they were to watch a miserable or emaciated bear pacing up and down on the concrete floor of a cage. In addition to observing rescued bears, visitors may be able to visit an educational centre at the sanctuary where they can read information panels and watch video material to further their understanding of bears, the threats they face, their natural biology, and the need for the protection of wild animals and their environments.

The Romanian bear sanctuary

I N FEBRUARY 1998, A REPRESENTATIVE from the London office of the World Society for the Protection of Animals (WSPA) travelled to Romania to meet with animal welfare groups and government representatives. This was part of a European-wide assessment of problems affecting the welfare of animals.

One of the main issues concerning the local animal groups in Romania at that time was the poor treatment of thousands of abandoned stray dogs left to roam the streets of the towns and cities. The methods used by local authorities to control the stray dog population often led to severe suffering. Many of the dogs were being poisoned on the streets or collected and kept in appalling overcrowded conditions before being euthanized by crude methods.

One of the Romanian animal groups trying to improve the situation was the 'Asociatia Milioane de Prieteni', or 'Millions of Friends', run by a Romanian woman called Cristina Lapis, who was the society's President. Cristina had spent her life caring for animals and with the help of her friend Brigitte Bardot she had set up a dog shelter near her home town of Brasov, in the heart of Transylvania, and was battling with the local authorities over the ill-treatment of stray dogs.

While the WSPA representative was in Brasov to meet Cristina to discuss the stray dog problem, he also suggested they make a visit to a nearby town called Poiana Brasov to look at some captive bears. The WSPA had been investigating animal welfare issues affecting captive bears around the world since 1992, when the organisation had created its 'Libearty' campaign aimed at 'Protecting bears from cruelty in captivity and in the wild'. The campaign had attracted international interest and reports of bears held in poor captive conditions around the world were regularly sent to the WSPA from the general public. In this case, tourists visiting the ski resort above Poiana Brasov had reported seeing bears suffering in small cages outside a restaurant in the area.

On visiting the town, Cristina was horrified to see three adult brown bears in small rusted cages in an area behind the restaurant. The bears were in a miserable condition with no shelter from the heat of the summer or the rain and snow of the harsh Romanian winter. Restaurant scraps were the only food source and the bears were clearly in a state of poor physical and mental health. The bears were named Cristi, Lydia and Viorel. This visit proved to be the pivotal point which eventually led to the creation of the Romanian bear sanctuary.

The WSPA had also received reports from tourists who had seen a bear paraded in public on the end of a chain in the touristic town of Sinaia, 50 km south of Brasov. Again, Cristina went to see for herself and was shocked to see the young bear being dragged around for tourist snapshots.

above: Cristina Lapis, President of the Romanian animal Group 'Millions of Friends'.

opposite page: Bears kept illegally in cages.

From that day on Cristina vowed to help the captive bears of Romania. She would lobby the Romanian authorities to release the bears from their captivity, but where could they go? The zoos in Romania were overcrowded and the conditions for bears in most of these zoos were little better than in the rusted restaurant cages.

At that time, the WSPA was at the fore-front of an international campaign to protect bears from cruelty around the world and had initiated projects to rescue dancing bears from the streets in Greece and Turkey and from cruel bear-baiting competitions in Pakistan. The principal tool for ensuring success had been an innovative idea developed by the WSPA – the bear sanctuary.

Before the WSPA had come up with the idea of the bear sanctuary, any bears which were rescued or removed from illegal trade anywhere in the world were invariably placed into cages in rescue centres or put into zoos. The WSPA, through its Libearty campaign, showed that it was possible to create a natural, forested enclosure of sufficient size to allow rescued bears to live out their lives in a protected wild environment where they would be free to climb trees, swim in large pools, dig in the earth and hibernate naturally, often for the first time in their lives.

The WSPA, working with a newly created Greek animal group, built the world's first bear sanctuary in Greece in 1993 to enable the Greek authorities to enforce the law and confiscate all the dancing bears used on the streets. All the rescued bears were released into a large enclosed area of forest in the north of Greece. The sanctuary enclosure was protected by a tall electrified fence to prevent the bears escaping or people and wild bears from getting in. A new Greek environmental organisation called

Arcturos was created to help build the sanctuary and oversee its management for the future.

In 1994 the WSPA built a bear sanctuary in Turkey to help the authorities eradicate dancing bears there. By 1998 they were busy building bear sanctuaries in Thailand and were also planning others in India and Pakistan.

The rescued bears could not be released back to the wild either because of their age, damage to teeth and claws, or because they had become so accustomed to people that they might approach human settlements.

Was there a need to build a sanctuary for bears in Romania? For 3 or 4 bears it would not be worth considering due to the expense, so for the moment this was not an option, but were there other bears in similar conditions in Romania? Cristina wanted to find out if the situation of the bears at Poiana Brasov was a one-off problem or if there was a larger issue of captive bear welfare to investigate.

Cristina and her husband Roger Lapis were so concerned for the welfare of the caged bears that they regularly went to check on them, taking food and even taking vets to treat the bears. The restaurant owner in Poiana Brasov was feeding them less often and never seemed to be aware of the poor health of the animals.

Another bear was found in a cage outside a restaurant in the small town of Bran, which attracted tourists to its famous Dracula Castle. The bear, called Maia, was in a particularly poor condition and was self mutilating – she was biting her limbs badly causing bleeding and infections. This was very likely to have been due to the poor mental condition of the animal because of its confinement in such barren conditions. Wild animals such as bears need vast open areas of forest to be able to use their natural foraging behaviour. In small cages, such as in many zoos, they often end up showing some form of abnormal behaviour such as pacing up

and down continuously, or even rocking from side to side. Some animals in these situations turn to self mutilation showing they have serious mental anxieties.

Cristina brought a vet many times to try and treat Maia, even putting a neck collar on her to try to stop her from chewing on her limbs, but the bear lost weight and died. Cristina wanted to prevent any more bears from going through such torment in captivity and only a bear sanctuary could offer these persecuted bears their freedom from suffering.

For the next few years the WSPA would be busy working on bear sanctuaries in India and Pakistan, to take care of bears rescued from the dancing bear and bear-baiting trade in those countries. But by 2004, news of more bears being held in cages in Romania was coming to light. Cristina Lapis was gathering a list of locations where captive bears were being kept, and the WSPA also enlisted the support of another local Romanian animal group called the Association for the Protection of Animals in Romania (APAR) who travelled around the country documenting where bears were being kept in cages.

There were at least 40 bears being kept illegally outside restaurants, petrol stations, near ski resorts and also in people's back yards. Photos of these bears showed clear evidence of their poor health and living conditions.

It was against Romanian law to take a bear from the wild and to keep it in private hands. The only captive bears allowed were those in recognised zoos. But over the years a lot of bear cubs had been 'found' or rather caught from the wild and had turned up in cages here and there and no action had so far been taken to prevent it. As for the zoos, there were 40 zoos dotted around the country and the majority were in a poor state with little funding to cover proper management, let alone proper care of the animals, and there were bears in most of the zoos.

It was clear that there was a need to persuade the Romanian government to take action against the illegal keeping of bears, but that could only succeed if there was somewhere to re-home the confiscated bears. None of the captive bears could be released back to the wild as there are too many problems associated with the rehabilitation of bears which have been kept for so long in such poor living conditions, and the zoos already had more bears than they could deal with. The only solution was to build a bear sanctuary.

In 2004, Peter Davies, the then Director General of the WSPA, visited Romania and was shown a bear in particularly poor captive conditions. The 12 year old female bear had spent her life in a wire cage measuring 2 metres square. The cage was open to the elements and her diet consisted almost entirely of corn, as the bear was kept on a maize farm.

The bear was in a miserable condition but had survived the years of hardship due to the resilience of these animals to the worst of situations. Peter was convinced that the WSPA should support a project to create a bear sanctuary in Romania.

In early 2005 a partnership was formed between Cristina Lapis's Milioane De Prieteni organisation and the World Society for the Protection of Animals with the aim of creating a bear sanctuary to eradicate the cruel treatment of captive bears in Romania. Cristina's organisation would oversee the construction of the

above and left: Bears were kept in appalling conditions, with little consideration given to their welfare.

sanctuary and the rescue of the bears, and the WSPA would supply the funding and technical expertise to design the sanctuary and advise on the rescue and care of the bears.

But one major element was missing. To create the sanctuary, a large area of forested

above: Brasov city.

land would be needed which had a year-round natural water supply, good road access and a nearby electricity supply. Although there is plenty of suitable forest in Romania, very little is actually available to use for such projects.

After several months of searching, the options had been narrowed down to 3 areas of forest within a 30 minute drive of Brasov. Of these areas, the best forest and the best offer came from the municipality of Zarnesti, a small town nestled against the southern Carpathian mountains, 25 km south of the city of Brasov.

The Mayor of Zarnesti at that time was a large jovial man named Gheorghe Lupu. Although the mayors of other regions nearby had not seen any benefit in having 50 bears living in a forest sanctuary near to their town, Mayor Lupu saw the potential for bringing jobs and tourists to Zarnesti.

He was all too aware of the many tourists who passed by Zarnesti on their way to the nearby town of Bran where the mega-tourist attraction of Dracula Castle drew half a million visitors annually. The problem was that once the tourists had visited the castle and then bought their Dracula T-shirts and souvenirs in the town of Bran, they got back on their tour bus and sped past Zarnesti on their way to their next tourist destination, the city of Brasov.

Once the bear sanctuary had rescued all the captive bears, the plan was to create a wildlife education centre at the site to create public awareness of the need to protect Romania's wildlife. Visitors would be able to see the bears in their new forest home splashing about in the pools, climbing trees or just lazing around in the meadows. Having the sanctuary just outside the town could benefit the local community by encouraging tourists to stop off in Zarnesti's shops, cafés and hotels before zooming off to Brasov.

The mayor was keen to support the project and said he had the perfect site. A couple of minutes drive out of the town a small side road

The plan was to create a wildlife education centre at the site to create public awareness of the need to protect Romania's wildlife.

veered off the main Zarnesti to Brasov road and after passing over a rickety bridge it wound up the steep hillside. The road was mainly used by shepherds as the hillside meadows were traditional sheep pastures.

Two kilometres higher up the hill the road ended in front of a large forest of oak and hazel trees. The perfect site for a bear sanctuary. At least 20 hectares of land would be needed to construct the sanctuary enclosures and necessary buildings, but the mayor drew up an agreement with the Milioane de Prieteni to provide the bear sanctuary with a 69 hectare (160 acre) area of the forest for the next 49 years. This gave the project enough space to pick and choose the best sites for each forest enclosure and would also ensure more enclosures could be built in the future if needed.

below: Map of Europe showing Zarnesti.

Building the sanctuary

A BEAR SANCTUARY HAS TO HAVE CERTAIN features. The main area is the forested enclosures in which the bears live for the rest of their lives. There may be one or more securely fenced enclosures, each measuring several hectares in size and containing natural forest and scrub habitat. Fresh water pools have to be created inside the enclosures to allow the bears to swim and cool off in hot weather. Dens are created to allow the bears to rest away from other bears or to hibernate in during winter months.

The main sanctuary buildings have to include quarantine dens for newly rescued bears, a veterinary clinic, food storage and preparation areas and staff quarters.

Paul Hammond was brought in to design the Romanian bear sanctuary enclosures and buildings. Paul was a specialist in working with captive wild animals and had spent many years working with zoos and wildlife projects around the world. He had worked with the WSPA designing bear sanctuaries in Thailand and India, and had also worked on improving the bear sanctuaries in Turkey and Pakistan. The Romanian bear sanctuary was to be one of the largest ever created and it would be expensive to build.

Roger Lapis, Cristina's husband, undertook the daily management of the work to build the sanctuary. He organised the local workforce and ordered the necessary machinery, equipment and construction materials. Roger was born in France and had worked as an engi-

neer managing a number of companies before settling down in Romania, where he met his future wife, Cristina. Roger now occupied the position of Honorary French Consul for Brasov and he, like Cristina, was committed to helping the captive bears.

The job of managing the sanctuary staff and overseeing the care of the bears was given to an enthusiastic man and wife team – Lotzi and Emi Dinka, who took on the difficult task of organising the rescue work and ensuring that the care of the rescued animals was the priority of the sanctuary.

The first task in the creation of the Zarnesti bear sanctuary was to make the entire 69 hectare perimeter of the forest secure. The sanctuary forest was part of a larger forest which stretched into the Carpathian Mountains and it was perfect natural bear habitat. In fact, wild bears were known to come through the forests around the sanctuary site so it was certainly going to be a great home for the once-caged bears.

There was plenty of natural food with the abundance of acorns and hazelnuts in the autumn and a variety of other plants and berries throughout the year. Of course, the bears would need to be given a lot of extra food to supplement their diet. In the wild, a European brown bear would normally have a territory extending 20 km or more in which they would roam continuously in search of different food sources. But the bears in the forest sanctuary would be

above: Roger Lapis planned the pathways through the forest.

content with their restricted forest area as long as there was sufficient food available.

The forest had also been used in recent years by local gypsies who stole wood for building timber and firewood. They would come in with their horses and carts and cut down trees which, although illegal, was difficult to monitor so high up in the hills. The sanctuary area now had to be protected from wandering gypsies so Roger Lapis erected a barbed wire boundary fence around the whole of the 69 hectares. Inside this area there would eventually be several enclosures for the bears, each measuring 6 to 8 hectares in size, and these would be surrounded by high weld-mesh fences protected by electric wires.

But the boundary fence did not work at first. The gypsies were well-known for using any piece of wood, metal or wire they came across, and soon there were gaps in the fencing where the barbed wire had been cut and taken for some other use, and the horses and carts then simply went through into the forest and returned home laden with fresh wood.

Roger had to fortify the boundary fence, so a deep ditch was dug in front of the barbed wire fence all along the perimeter. This worked. The horses and carts could not cross and were blocked, leaving the gypsies to search elsewhere for their wood.

The next step was to build a gravelled road-way through the forest to the centre, where the main building would be situated. This building would be the heart of the sanctuary and would contain a number of quarantine dens, a veterinary clinic, food storage and preparation rooms and staff working areas. The forested bear enclosures would all lead to this building.

The route for the roadway was planned and started, only to come to an immediate halt when the JCB diggers suddenly found huge metal pipes just a metre under the ground. These turned out to be two large trans-national gas pipes which traversed Hungary, Romania and Bulgaria and just happened to run straight through the forest above Zarnesti. They were not on the detailed plans supplied by the local authorities and no one seemed to know they were there, but the local mayor was pleased they had been found and their location was mapped, recorded and filed away in the municipality's record office. The sanctuary roadway and main building were re-sited, carefully avoiding the path of the pipes, and work restarted.

By late summer 2005 work on the roadways and foundations for the first main sanctuary enclosure fence were well underway. The aim was to finish the first enclosure and the main building with its quarantine dens and vet clinic by the end of 2006 and to then start confiscating the first bears, but other events intervened and led to an emergency rescue of bears.

Building the Zarnesti Sanctuary

Paul Hammond designed the buildings and the sanctuary enclosures which were to become home to over 50 rescued bears.

Roger checking the layout of the site plan.

Weld mesh fences fitted with electric wire enclose the sanctuary.

Building the tall weld mesh fences of the bear sanctuary forest enclosure.

Large freshwater pools were created for the bears to swim and cool off in during the hot summer months.

Dens were constructed to encourage the bears to hibernate during the winter.

Finally the day arrived everyone had worked so hard for – the sanctuary's first bears, Cristi and Lydia, are released into their new home.

2005 – The first bears

THE FIRST BEAR BROUGHT TO THE sanctuary was a gentle giant, named Cristi. He was also one of the major inspirations behind the creation of the Romanian bear sanctuary.

In 1981 Cristi was bought as a cub by the owner of a restaurant in the town of Poiana Brasov. This town is 12 km north of Brasov and higher up in the mountains in the heart of Tran-

sylvania. Due to its high altitude the area gets a lot of snow during the long winter and it has developed into a major ski resort with tourists from Romania and abroad flocking to the ski runs high up in the Carpathian Mountains.

Cristi had been caught from the wild, probably after his mother had been killed by hunters. The owner kept Cristi in a small cage behind his restaurant to attract more customers who

left: Cristi in the mini-zoo cage.
right: The mini-zoo sign at Poiana Brasov.

would come to see the young bear and feed him scraps of food.

Cristi lived alone in his cage of iron bars and concrete floor for the first 10 years of his life until the restaurant owner acquired another bear, a female, which he named Lydia. Tourists now had to pay a small fee to see the bears so for a while the bears brought in extra income for the owner. The two bears shared less than 20 square metres of concrete floor with nothing to occupy their naturally lively minds and only restaurant scraps as food. They would sit on the concrete freezing throughout the long winters and suffocating in the heat of the Romanian summers.

In such a small living area the bears often snapped at each other, Lydia being more belligerent, and Cristi usually trying to escape confrontation. But in a small cage, as in many zoo enclosures, there is no escape and the psychological stress on animals kept in such conditions can be enormous.

Over the years the restaurant owner paid less attention to his bears and hardly fed them. Fewer people paid to see the two pitiful animals in their rusting cage. They survived mainly from food given them by the few tourists who ventured behind the run-down restaurant past a dilapidated 'Mini-Zoo' sign. The only other animals in a nearby rusted cage were some rabbits and chickens.

Cristi was no longer the cute cub and had grown to be a giant of a bear. His fur was dark and his massive head and paws showed he

would have become a magnificent dominant bear if he had been able to live a natural life in the mountains of his birth. Lydia was much smaller than Cristi. Female brown bears are typically a third smaller than males, and in contrast to Cristi's dark pelt she had very light fur. Although they are called brown bears, their fur can vary from black to very fair.

Cristi and Lydia lived a pathetic existence in the cage, but in 1998 an officer from the World Society for the Protection of Animals made a visit to Romania to investigate the awful stray dog situation and to respond to a number of complaints received by WSPA head office regarding some captive bears next to a restaurant in Poiana Brasov.

The WSPA officer met with the restaurant owner and brought a representative from a newly formed animal protection group in Brasov to assess the situation. That representative was Cristina Lapis, who had recently set up a dog shelter in Brasov. She was shocked to see the bears kept in such miserable conditions and from that day she vowed to see the bears set free.

From the first day Cristina and her husband Roger saw the misery of Cristi and Lydia they made regular visits to the cages bringing food for the bears, always in the hope that one day they could be rescued.

The construction of the bear sanctuary began in early 2005, but in July 2005 Cristina was told that the restaurant in Poiana Brasov was going to be demolished and the bears were

going to be killed as the owner had nowhere to put them. The bear sanctuary was still in very early stages of construction, with roads being built into the Zarnesti forest area and the first stages of the large fenced enclosure underway.

But the situation was desperate so Cristina's team rapidly built a few quarantine cages on the perimeter of the sanctuary site and organised a legal confiscation of Cristi and Lydia and another bear called Odi, who by then had been moved to the restaurant cages from a small farm hundreds of kilometres away.

On a baking hot day in August 2005, the sanctuary team drove a lorry to Poiana Brasov in time to see the remains of the restaurant being knocked down. The bears in their cages were covered in dust and were clearly stressed by the noise and confusion surrounding them. Each bear was enticed into a transport cage and whisked back to the sanctuary on the back of the lorry. It had been a tense time and a very lucky escape for the bears, but now they were about to start their new lives in the sanctuary forest.

The first bears had arrived at the sanctuary.

Although the quarantine dens were small, the rescued bears appeared content to be given clean, warm straw to sleep on and plenty of nourishing food. They would have to stay in this area over the winter period but once their dens were packed up with warm straw they had no trouble sleeping for much of the winter and the bears hibernated, probably for the first time in their lives.

Romanian winters can be harsh and, as the ground froze and a thick blanket of snow covered the forest, the work on the sanctuary slowed down but did not stop completely. The noise of the trucks carrying tons of gravel for the access road and the JCB digger, which for months had been relentlessly excavating a 1 metre deep trench around the one and a half kilometre perimeter of the first forest enclosure, all came to a halt. The only sounds which remained were the scratchy squawks of crows and, if you listened carefully, the gentle snoring of snoozing bears in their hibernation dens.

opposite page: Lydia in the mini-zoo cage.
below: Rescue – on the way to the sanctuary.
right: Offloading bear and cage at the sanctuary.
bottom: Safe in quarantine at the Zarnesti sanctuary.

2006 – First bear enclosure

A S SOON AS THE SNOWS HAD MELTED THE following spring, work re-commenced to build the first large sanctuary enclosure, but it was decided to also create a smaller forest enclosure which could be built quickly to allow Cristi and Lydia out of the quarantine dens.

A few months later the first rescued bears set paw into the forest. Cristi and Lydia had lived in the same cramped cage behind a restaurant for over 14 years before being rescued and brought to the sanctuary. They had become inseparable and had even hibernated together in a deep nest of straw in the sanctuary's quarantine den. They would be able to live together without any problem in the new small forest enclosure, which had a fresh water pool and

a den dug into the ground with a roof of tree trunks and branches.

The release of the bears into the new 1.5 hectare forest enclosure was to be a major event and Cristina and Roger were there along with Paul Hammond, who had made the trip to Zarnesti to double check the enclosure and the electric fencing to ensure everything was ready for the bears.

Lydia was the first to be released. She was enticed out of the warm quarantine den into a transport cage which was then carried by the JCB vehicle down the gravel roadway into the forest area. Her cage was secured in place against the gate into the forest enclosure and the gates to the cage and enclosure were lifted.

All bears react differently when it comes to moving them from cage to large open forest. Each bear has its own character, its likes and dislikes, and each has its own fears and frustrations. When suddenly faced with an open door into a seemingly endless space of earth, grass, trees and the myriad of sights, sounds and smells of a forest, it is not surprising that an animal

left: The oak forest site where the sanctuary enclosures were built.
opposite page: Lydia and Cristi, explore their new home.

After living together for 14 years, Cristi and Lydia had become inseparable – they had even hibernated together in the sanctuary's quarantine den.

which has spent its entire life in a concrete and iron barred cage is a little unsure about stepping out into the unknown. After all, in many cases the cage is all the bear has known. It has been its home and despite the lack of space and natural comforts, the cage has represented a sort of security. So, faced with an apparently endless horizon of grass and forest, the bear is very likely to show some initial signs of stress and confusion.

Although it may seem strange, some bears which have spent their life in a small cage initially appear to have a fear of open spaces. They look out through the small door of their cage into the vast open forest and rather than eagerly stepping out into such an enriched

environment, they sometimes prefer to peer at it all from the safety of their cage.

It can take a few hours, even a few days, before a bear will put one tentative paw then another onto the grass in front of the cage and step out into its new world. Sometimes some tasty food thrown in front of the cage door will entice the bear out. Sometimes it just takes time.

On other occasions the bear may race out of the cage as soon as the door is opened. Lydia raced out, but 5 metres from the cage she stopped dead and turned and looked back to the perimeter fence behind which the sanctuary staff were watching. As if all her senses were suddenly on overload, Lydia started sniffing the grass between her paws, she clawed at the earth and forgot about the people who, just a few metres away, were now cheering and snapping photos of the first bear to be released into the Romanian bear sanctuary. Lydia walked slowly onwards through the grass, sniffing at the bushes and even tasting the leaves as she passed by some hazel bushes. She would be fine. The first release had been a success.

Cristi was next, and the huge bear happily lumbered out of the cage and walked through the grass as if in a dream, slowly putting down one huge paw after another on the springy grass as if testing the surprising new floor of his forest home, while swinging his huge head from side to side sniffing at everything around him.

Cristi and Lydia, like most of the bears kept in cages in Romania, had been caught from the wild at a few months of age. Their mothers were almost certainly killed by hunters so they had no time to experience their natural environment in the rich forest of the Carpathian Mountains. It is difficult to imagine how a bear must feel when it is released back into a forest, after so many years living in such unnatural,

empty and undoubtedly stressful and painful conditions. It may be frightening at first, it may be stressful, but it very quickly becomes a paradise for the once-captive bears.

The spring and summer of 2006 was a busy time at the sanctuary. Work continued on the first large forest enclosure. Two huge fresh water pools had to be constructed for the bears to cool off in during the very hot summers, and a number of dens were built from earth and wood to encourage the bears to hibernate in winter.

The enclosure covered 7 hectares (around 17 acres) of rich oak forest and the 2.5 metre high perimeter fence that surrounded the enclosure ran for one and a half kilometres, with over ten kilometres of multi stranded electric wires protecting the inside of the fence. It was a big job and Roger Lapis was careful to try to protect as many trees as possible, so the fence had to run around a tree rather than have the tree felled to make way for the fence.

But there were many obstacles to overcome. The cost of wood, concrete, petrol and electricity were rising sharply and the Romanian currency (the Romanian Lei) was losing value against the US Dollar and the Euro.

The local authorities decided that there had to be a fire suppression unit created at the sanctuary. This was basically several huge tanks buried in the ground to contain a water supply to be used in case of fire in the forest. Electricity had to be brought all the way up the two kilometre roadway from Zarnesti to the top of the sanctuary hill. The roadway into the sanctuary had to have dozens of truckloads of gravel laid down to create an access road. All these things added to the cost and took time to complete. Meanwhile the foundations for the large main building were ready and the walls and roof needed to be finished.

Although the main enclosure would not be ready until the end of the year, there were urgent cases of bears needing to be rescued. Mura, a 5 year old female bear had been used as a performing bear in the 'Globus Circus' in Bucharest. She had been made to ride a bicycle, wear a child's skirt and walk around on her hind paws. One day Mura simply refused to perform.

The circus owners beat her and starved her but still the bear wouldn't respond.

It seems that the circus owner finally took pity on the small bear and decided not to keep punishing her but to try to find her a new home. He had heard of the bear sanctuary so he called Cristina Lapis to ask if she would accept Mura at the sanctuary.

Cristina took the bear and made the circus owner promise not to use bears in his circus in future. Mura was brought to the quarantine area at the Zarnesti bear sanctuary where she recuperated for a few months. When she was eventually released into the main forested area she quickly learned the joys of climbing trees and swimming in the pool with other bears. The suffering of her circus days were over.

An 11 year old female bear called Suzi was rescued from a small enclosure in a run-down zoo. She had spent her first 4 years in a circus

and then was given to the zoo. Suzi was a particularly nervous bear and when she was released into the sanctuary's forest enclosure she found a tree close to the fence and stayed there for 2 months. She would pace up and down from the tree to the fence and up to 2 metres each side, but no further. If she was frightened by any noise, she would race to the tree and, getting up on her hind paws, she would hug the tree for comfort.

It was clear that this bear was actually afraid of the open space of the forest and used the tree and fence as if they were the imaginary boundaries of her small zoo cage in which she was held captive for so many years. Nothing would entice her away from her safe tree. The sanctuary staff tried throwing food further away from her tree but she would walk just so far and then appear to reach an invisible wall, and go no further. Fortunately, after a couple of months, one day she suddenly walked outside of her comfort zone and kept walking, having found the large forest not to be so frightening after all. She was soon seen mixing with other bears and had no further problems.

Gina & Sophia

THE FUNDING FOR SUCH A MASSIVE PROJECT was mainly the responsibility of the World Society for the Protection of Animals, who relied on the goodwill of their thousands of supporters around the world for donations to such projects. Another way to raise funds was to get wider public awareness of the project through media stories.

On an overcast day in October 2006 the bear sanctuary team was tearing along the road heading north out of Brasov. The bear sanctuary team were in the main vehicle carrying the transport cage, and two cars followed on behind.

The British newspaper, the *Sunday Mirror*, had sent a journalist to Romania to report on a bear rescue. They brought with them Dominic Brunt, a British actor who plays a veterinarian in a popular TV soap series called *Emmerdale*. Dominic was already a WSPA supporter and was making this visit to see for himself how captive bears were being rescued from a miserable life. His presence at the bear rescue would also enhance the public interest in the news story.

The plan was to rescue a bear called Baloo, who had been kept in a cage near a restaurant in the town of Bancu Miercurea in Central Romania. All bears taken to the sanctuary have to be legally confiscated. The Romanian Ministry of Environment has to draw up a legal document stating that the bear is being confiscated and given into the care of the bear sanctuary.

above: Baloo in her rusty cage at the mini-zoo.
top: Actor Dominic Brunt is shocked to see the poor condition of Baloo's cage.

Cristina Lapis had been trying to get the legal authority to confiscate this bear for some time and a few days earlier the necessary paperwork had been approved. A quarantine cage had been made ready at the sanctuary and they were ready to move.

Back on the road – after 2 hours of driving along good roads the convoy of vehicles turned off onto a series of dusty side roads and past a small village. Cristina had arranged to meet the local representative of the Ministry of Environment outside the mini zoo. He had brought the official paperwork with him to enforce the legal confiscation of the bear.

The sanctuary vehicles drove through the gates and were confronted by several rows of run down sheds and cages. Luckily there were no public visitors that day. The mini-zoo owner was there – a very large man using a quad bike to get around. The man from the Ministry confronted him and told him in no uncertain terms that the animals at the mini-zoo were being kept there illegally and the bear was to be removed.

While this was going on the sheds were searched and Baloo was found. The poor bear was about 4 years old, thin and ragged looking. Her cage was small and dirty with no sign of food. As the transport cage was moved into position next to Baloo's cage Lotzi came back

left: Gina and Sophia in the mini-zoo.

They were bear cubs, caught from the wild that year soon after they were born and by now were around 8 months old.

from searching the site with bad news. There were 2 large adult bears in another cage.

Worse was to come. The owner, now angry about the raid, was complaining to the Ministry officer and was unsuccessfully arguing that all his animals were legally owned. Even the young bears, he said, banging his fist on an old shed. There was a rustle from inside the shed and two furry heads appeared at a small barred window. They were bear cubs, caught from the wild earlier that year soon after they were born and by now were around 8 months old.

The owner said the cubs were saved by the mini-zoo as they were found in the wild and brought there, otherwise they would have died. The truth is more likely to be that he bought them from a hunter. The law in Romania forbids the private keeping of wild animals such as bears and this mini-zoo did not have any legal permit to keep such animals. The cubs would also be confiscated and taken to the sanctuary.

The owner, clearly annoyed but resigned to the fact that he was being given no choice, went to the shed and flicked open the door then drove off on his bike.

Two lively bear cubs bounded out into the sunlight and raced around between everyone's legs. Paying visitors to the mini-zoo would have fed and petted these cubs, who appeared to have been regularly released into the public areas for tourists to take photos. While they were 3 or 4 months old they would have been like cute living teddy bears, but these cubs were now 8 months old and were big enough and strong enough to seriously injure someone. By this age they are powerful animals, armed with very sharp teeth and claws, and even if a cub only meant to play it could easily inflict a serious wound on someone.

But for the moment the cubs were just eager to race around and explore the grass, the other cages, and especially the people. Cristina was in tears at first, knowing that the cubs' mother had probably been killed to get the cubs. But as they played around her feet she offered them some fruit and they calmed down for a moment before racing off again. They wrestled peoples' legs but did no damage and they were soon tired out and easily enticed back into their shed.

above left: Gina and Sophia at the mini-zoo.
opposite page: Pierre Brice and the Mayor of Zarnesti taking the traditional welcome of bread and salt.

So the sanctuary team had a problem. They had come all this way to pick up one bear and had brought just one transport cage. All of the bears now had to be taken to the sanctuary so it would mean several return trips.

As the original aim was to rescue Baloo, she was the first to go. After strapping the sanctuary's transport cage to the rusted cage of Baloo,

Emi knelt down and spoke softly to the anxious bear while offering tasty food to tempt her into the smaller cage. Everyone else stood back, away from the area, to ensure the bear could calm down.

Emi was working her usual miracle with the bears. Baloo was becoming calmer listening to her reassuring voice and within 15 minutes had

stepped into the transport cage and the door was dropped and bolted.

It was a long day for the team. They raced back to the sanctuary and put Baloo into a quarantine cage, gave her plenty of food and then turned around and drove for 3 hours back to the mini-zoo for the cubs.

By the next morning the two female cubs, most probably sisters, were safe in the quarantine cages of the sanctuary. They were far too small to put into the forest enclosure so they would have to spend the winter in the temporary quarantine area.

A month later, in November 2006, Cristina Lapis decided to have an inauguration of the sanctuary. Although there was still a long way to go to finish the construction work and rescue all the bears, there was at least one large and one small enclosure already occupied by several rescued bears and the main sanctuary building had its foundations laid, the walls and framework were up, and now the roof had just been erected.

The purpose of the inauguration was to gain the support of the Romanian government and media for the ongoing rescue of captive bears, and also to show them what had been achieved so far. The government had been supportive in providing the necessary legal paperwork to confiscate the bears but they had no funding to offer the project. Cristina was hopeful that the Ministry of Transport would at least help to improve the pot-holed road leading

from Zarnesti up the hill to the sanctuary, so the Minister for Transport was also invited to the event.

The Romanian media had already taken the bear sanctuary to its heart and had publicised the rescue of the first bears on many TV and radio channels, as well as in newspaper stories. The media was a powerful friend for the project and this event was another chance to feed them a newsworthy story.

Cristina had also invited a friend to the event, Pierre Brice, who was a famous film star

When they grew tired, they would both climb a tree, often the same tree, and sleep in the branches.

of French and German cinema. He was famous for his roles as a fictional Apache Chief called Winnetou in eleven German Western movies in the 1960s and he continued this famous role in TV documentaries and mini series up until the 1990s.

These films had also been popular in Romania so Pierre was quite a celebrity to the Romanian public and his attendance at the bear sanctuary event was certain to increase the media's interest.

Sure enough, on the day of the bear sanctuary inauguration, a swarm of cars headed up the hill containing TV and radio reporters from around the country. Some local dignitaries and even a Government Minister were among them.

The Mayor of Zarnesti, Gheorghe Lupu, together with Cristina Lapis, Pierre Brice and Victor Watkins from WSPA were waiting at the entrance to the sanctuary forest to welcome them. The visitors were presented with bread and salt by young women dressed in colourful national costume, in accordance with an age-old Romanian custom of offering a welcome gift of the basic necessities of life.

The TV stations throughout Romania were full of the story that day, reporting with pride on the new Romanian bear sanctuary. Pierre Brice featured in innumerable interviews and was overjoyed to see the two newly rescued female cubs who he promptly named Gina and Sophia, after his actress friends Gina Lollobrigida and Sophia Loren.

Curiously, Sophia has a cleft lip. When people first see her close up, they think her lip has been torn by having a ring put through it, as they do with dancing bears in other countries, but it is in fact just how she was born, and although it looks rather odd it doesn't seem to affect her health nor her voracious appetite.

With winter approaching, Gina and Sophia hibernated in their quarantine den. Later on they would move into a 1 hectare forest enclosure next to Cristi and Lydia. The yearling cubs loved the freedom of the forest and spent their days chasing after each other and splashing in the pool. When they grew tired, they would both climb a tree, often the same tree, and sleep in the branches. From their high vantage point they could see Lotzi and Emi arriving with fresh fruit and vegetables each day and they were always waiting eagerly near the fence for their feast, both wailing pitifully to persuade Emi to feed them.

When the winter snows fell on the oak forest sanctuary in November 2006, the rescued bears Cristi and Lydia slept together in their wood and earth den in the forest enclosure and a blanket of snow slowed construction work until the following spring.

Although Cristina was pleased that seventeen bears had been rescued and brought to the sanctuary by the end of 2006, she continuously worried about the many bears still remaining in terrible conditions.

2007 – Zoo closures

2007 TURNED OUT TO BE A MOMENTOUS year for Romania. On January 1st 2007 Romania became a member of the European Union (EU). After years of lobbying and preparation, the country became the 27th member of the EU amidst public celebrations in Bucharest and throughout the country. Membership of the EU offered the country a huge step forward in the creation of more jobs, more trade and foreign investment.

But there were also many problems to overcome, including how to adjust to new EU laws. One of these laws was the EU Zoo Directive which stipulates that all EU member countries have to bring the management of their zoos up to a certain standard.

In 2007 there were 41 zoos in Romania. Around 20 of those zoos were members of the Romanian Federation of Zoos which should mean they are well managed and provide reasonable living conditions for their animals. But the truth is that few of these zoos had been able to care for their animals sufficiently well. The animal enclosures were generally the old-fashioned concrete and barred cage design with no enrichment within to enable the animals to exhibit their natural behaviours.

Then of course there were the other 20 zoos in Romania that did not belong to the Romanian Zoo Federation. The conditions for animals in these places were often worse still.

The Romanian Zoo Federation had a serious problem. They had been well aware, before 2007,

that they had a lot of work to do in improving standards in their member zoos to comply with the forthcoming EU Zoo Directive. But little had been done and in 2007 they were faced with the awful truth that their zoos had to rapidly improve or else face closure.

There was some hope for these member zoos as they could get advice and help from the European Association of Zoos and Aquaria (EAZA), but the smaller and poorer zoos that were not members faced a real danger of closure.

One of Romania's animal protection organisations, called the Association for the Protection of Animals in Romania (APAR), had produced a report detailing every zoo in the country. It clearly showed the problems facing many of the zoos.

Animals were being kept in small, rusted and run-down enclosures, food for the animals

was inadequate and veterinary care was generally non-existent. The educational value of the zoos was in many cases considered to be negative as the visitors were shown captive wild animals with abnormal behaviours, due to their sterile environments.

Many zoos faced closure. Some of the animals had to be re-homed in the bigger and better managed zoos but it still left many animals faced with euthanasia. APAR, along with animal protection organisations such as the WSPA, Born Free Foundation and an Austrian group called Vier Pfoten, tried their best to help re-home some of the animals.

Some of the lions were sent to wildlife sanctuaries in Africa, others were moved around to other zoos in Romania. As for the bears, at least they were in luck, as the new bear sanctuary under construction near Brasov could take in these unfortunate animals and save them from death.

But there were a lot of bears, possibly 30 or more, in zoos that had to close down. The Zarnesti bear sanctuary had been designed to take around 40 bears which were known to be illegally kept in cages around the country. Now there were an extra 30 or more bears from zoos needing a home. Another forest enclosure would be needed and that would cost a lot more money to build and to maintain.

The WSPA decided it would find the extra funds and appealed to its supporters around the world, who responded positively. By late 2007

a second 7 hectare forest enclosure was being built but it would not be ready to take its first occupants until the spring of 2008.

During 2007 the first zoos started to close down, and the bear sanctuary team had to rush into action. They were appalled at the awful state of the bears kept in some of the zoos and it was amazing to think how the animals could have survived for so long in such terrible conditions.

Buhusi Zoo was a typical case. Buhusi is a small Romanian town 200 km north of Brasov. It used to be famous for having the biggest textile factory in south-eastern Europe but after the fall of Ceausescu in 1990, its business decreased and today there are only a small number of workers at the run-down factory.

Buhusi Zoo was one of only a few zoos in the north of the country and at one time it had been a popular attraction for the townspeople. But the Municipality had less and less money to spare and the zoo management deteriorated to the point where the animals started to die off while the remaining animals were kept alive on a meagre diet. It is unlikely that there had been any veterinary care there for many years.

In a desperate attempt to help the animals in Buhusi Zoo, a locally supported project called 'The Lion's Roar', created by American Laura Simms, had spent several years sending volunteers to feed the animals and trying to improve the environment for the few remaining animals. A few old lions still lived in barren rusty old cages. Some had hip and back defects from inbreeding and one lioness had a terrible case of glaucoma, making her left eye bulge like an opaque golf ball in the eye socket.

The remaining animals consisted of 5 bears, a few dingoes, a couple of monkeys and even a pair of domestic dogs, locked up in a small concrete and iron barred zoo enclosure next to the bears. These poor dogs, despite being caged, were desperate for attention and would bark at

passers by to attract them. Then with tails wagging furiously both dogs would frantically push their paws and sometimes their heads through the cage bars to get stroked by the people.

Conditions in Buhusi Zoo had become so bad that by early 2007 the government in Bucharest gave the order for the zoo to close down. The Zarnesti bear sanctuary was given permission to re-home the zoo bears and in April 2007 the sanctuary team made their first of 3 visits to the zoo to rescue them. There were 5 bears which needed to be taken to the sanctuary to prevent them from being euthanized. The state of the animals was shocking. They were underfed and kept in small, filthy concrete caged areas which gave no protection from the sun, rain or snow and it was clear that they had been in the cages for many years.

One of the bears, called Benny, was a 27 year old brown bear and had been in the same cage all of his life. He looked like a bag of bones. His eyes were weeping with infection and he was clearly starving. Ciprian, the bear sanctuary vet, could see the bear was old and frail and feared that if he had to tranquilise him to move him out of his rusted cage, the old bear may not survive the shock.

The cage looked like a dilapidated prison cell with its rusting barred front and crumbling concrete walls. Ciprian wanted to entice the old bear into the transport cage using food, rather than risk having to tranquilise him. But that meant opening up the gate to the old bear's

left to right: Benny, Ala and Ursula at Buhusi Zoo in their crumbling concrete enclosures.
above: Benny is finally tempted into the transport cage with a piece of chicken. Ala followed eventually after being unable to resist a pot of honey!

cage and attaching the transport cage to it. The gate was rusted solid as it had not been used for a decade or more.

Lotzi was always prepared for every eventuality and had brought a welding machine and a powerful circular saw and was soon cutting his way through the cage bars. With the transport cage finally attached, Emi began the patient task of trying to entice the old bear into the new cage. She used sweet cakes and fruit and even some meat. A piece of chicken was too much to resist and the starving old bear eventually stepped into the cage.

The next problem was to get the female bear called Ala into the second half of the transport cage. Ala had been Benny's partner for many years and had shared the small caged enclosure with him but she was younger and more anxious than old Benny and she refused to be tempted into the cage.

An hour passed, then two. The zoo manager came to try to help and he thought spraying the bear with a hose pipe would move her along. But Ala seemed to be quite pleased to have a cool shower in the heat of the day so that didn't work.

Then the weather started to deteriorate and rain was going to make it even more difficult to get Ala out of her enclosure. Ciprian was getting his dart gun ready as it looked as if there was no choice but to tranquilise her. But at the last minute, a small pot of honey was found and offered to the bear. It is true that all bears

love honey and Ala was no exception. Within minutes of her first taste of the honey, she was enticed into the transport cage and the gate was shut – the two bears were free.

With the bears safely back at the quarantine area of the bear sanctuary, Ciprian gave Benny some antibiotics mixed into a pot of honey. He was worried about the poor health of the old bear who also had a serious case of conjunctivitis. But over the following days both bears put on weight and their health improved. Ala would soon be able to move into the main forest enclosure but Benny was old and doddery and would not survive any threat from the younger male bears so he would have to stay in quarantine until a small forest area could be fenced off for him.

The sanctuary team went back to Buhusi to pick up two more brown bears and that left one remaining bear at the zoo. That bear was called Ursula and unlike the other rescued bears which were all European brown bears, Ursula was an Asiatic black bear. Her species is found in the wild in the forests of China, northern Japan and through Asia to India and Pakistan.

In the wild, Asiatic black bears enjoy lush tropical forest habitats and they spend much

left: Hansel and Gretel sitting back-to-back in the sanctuary.
opposite page: Benny at the sanctuary, looking healthy and well-fed.

of their time foraging over many kilometres of forest, climbing trees to eat the leaves and fruits and also sleeping in the trees, making nests from branches. But Ursula had spent part of her life with a Ukrainian circus and when she was no longer of any use to them they dumped her at Buhusi Zoo, where she was housed in a tiny concrete prison cell measuring 2 metres wide by 3 metres deep and 3 metres high. She had a concrete ledge to climb on and a small sleeping area underneath. No branches, no tree, no earth, only a small trough for water.

At 26 years of age, Ursula was an old bear. In the wild she would have lived for 20 years but probably not much more. In captivity bears can live longer but that often means they suffer for longer. Ursula was also partially blind. Her left eye was clouded by a cataract and her right eye seemed to be going the same way. The zoo could no longer look after her and would undoubtedly have put her to sleep if no other home was available. The Zarnesti bear sanctuary was her only hope but she was an old, nearly blind bear of a different species and the sanctuary had to consider how to care for her. It would not be until early the following year

that Ursula could be rescued, but more about that later.

Apart from the Buhusi Zoo bears, the sanctuary team were busy rescuing bears from other dilapidated zoos and private cages around the country. A zoo in a town called Calarasi, in the south of the country, had three bears needing rescuing. Two were brother and sister, named Hansel and Gretel. These 3 year old bears were kept in a darkened dungeon of a room, lit only by small light bulbs. Their father, a 24 year old bear called Ionica, was kept in a separate cage due to his old age.

The Calarasi Zoo used to be the pride of Romania and during the 1980s it was the largest zoo in the country. Part of its claim to fame was that it bred animals to sell to other zoos and even circuses. Now it could not even care for its animals and once again the bear sanctuary had to come to the rescue of caged bears to prevent them from being killed.

When Hansel and Gretel were eventually released into the bear sanctuary forest they immediately set about enjoying the new sights and smells. Hansel spent his time wandering through the thick forest vegetation while Gretel preferred the new experience of tree climbing and appeared even to enjoy sleeping high up in the branches, snoring softly. But no matter how far the bears each went on their explorations in the woods they still tended to find each other's company best and were often seen sitting back to back in the meadow areas.

Max, the blind bear

IN THE SUMMER OF 2008 A SMALL veterinary surgery on the outskirts of Brasov became the centre of attention for a host of Romanian TV cameramen and journalists – they had come to see a remarkable operation on a remarkable bear.

Max had spent the first 10 years of his life chained to railings for the entertainment of tourists. He was caught from the wild as a brown bear cub and used by his owner as a tourist attraction.

Max lived in a 4 metre square cage next to a small restaurant by night and each day he was dragged by a rope around his neck to some railings 10 metres away. That was his life. He walked 10 metres to and from his cage each day and spent the day chained to the railings where people would stop and take a photo of him, after paying for this souvenir snapshot.

Max was well known to the public as he was kept next to the road leading to one of the country's famous landmarks, the Peles Castle, which was built by King Carol I of Romania in the late 1800s. This magnificent castle regularly attracts crowds of tourists who have to walk up past the railings where Max was chained to reach the entrance to the castle grounds.

Many tourists could not resist taking a photo of this massive bear but few people realised the

right: Max chained and leaning on the railings.
opposite page: The cage where Max lived for 10 years and the railings, bent after years of him leaning on them.

cruelty of keeping a bear in this condition. In fact, the bear suffered not only from his poor captive conditions, he was also blind.

When the bear sanctuary was in the early stages of being built, undercover investigators visited Max and took photos of him chained to the railings. The bear's owner was furious when they refused to pay him for the photos and was aggressive and threatening. But Cristina Lapis vowed to rescue Max when the time was right.

By the summer of 2006 the sanctuary had its first forest enclosure ready and several bears

In quarantine, Max enjoyed a new
diet of fresh fruit and vegetables
and he quickly put on weight.

had been rescued. The Romanian government
fully supported the aim of confiscating all the
illegally held bears in the country and in September
2007 they sent the police, together with
officers from the National Guard of the Ministry
of Environment, to legally confiscate Max.
They needed the police to prevent the bear's
owner from obstructing the rescue.

A vet shot two tranquiliser darts into Max
while he was chained to the railings. Once
sedated, they cut his chains and loaded him into
a cage and took him away to start a new life.

Max was brought to the bear sanctuary but,
as he was blind, he needed special care and
attention. In the quarantine area he enjoyed a
new diet of fresh fruit and vegetables and he
quickly put on weight. Max was a giant of a
bear but he was a gentle and docile animal. He
got to know Emi's voice and would sit at the
front of his quarantine den to be fed like a child.
But everyone at the sanctuary wanted more for
Max. They wanted him to have a chance of
living in the forest, but was that possible?

During the summer of 2008 the WSPA
decided to take a chance and brought some specialists
to assess Max's eyes, to see if there was
any possibility of restoring his sight. It seemed
as if Max had cataracts but his eyes were cloudy
deep inside and each eye moved rapidly back
and forth all of the time.

By chance, a WSPA supporter in the UK had
called in with an amazing offer of help. She had
supported the WSPA for many years and said

that if there were any animals needing specialist
eye treatment, then her husband was the
man to call and he would volunteer his time if
needed.

That man turned out to be Dr. David Donaldson
who was the Head of a specialist veterinary
ophthalmology unit at the UK based
Animal Health Trust. David had operated on
wild animals as well as domestic pets and he
was one of few people capable of assessing Max
and possibly improving his eyesight.

WSPA's Wildlife Advisor, Victor Watkins,
wrote to David and explained about Max and
also sent him some close-up film footage to
show Max's eyes. David replied that the film
showed there was a serious problem with his
eyes but the only way to find out the extent of
the problem was to examine the bear.

David offered to visit the bear sanctuary
in Romania and do an assessment of Max and
operate on him if needed. This was not going to
be easy as any eye operation would have to be
done in a sterile and well equipped surgery and
the veterinary surgery at the bear sanctuary
was still under construction. It was decided that
to have any chance of performing the operation
Max would have to be brought to a veterinary
surgery in Brasov.

Dr. Liviu Harbuz, the Chief Veterinary Advisor
to the sanctuary, pulled out all the stops. He
really wanted to help Max and he persuaded a
friend who managed a modern veterinary surgery
in Brasov to let the eye specialists use his

surgery for a day. Liviu also brought several of Romania's top veterinary eye specialists from Bucharest University who would assist David Donaldson in the operation. This would be a unique learning experience for them as they normally only operated on dogs and cats. David also wanted to bring out with him two British specialists to help – Claudia Hartley, who was a fellow ophthalmologist, and Lizzie Leece, Head of Anaesthesiology at the British Animal Health Trust.

Weeks passed as preparations were made, then in July 2008 the British and Romanian teams converged on Zarnesti. Max was enticed out of his quarantine den into the transport cage, ready to be taken to the veterinary clinic 25 km away in Brasov. This gave David and Claudia a chance to examine the bear but they needed to have a good look into his eyes and with Max shuffling nervously around inside the cage it was an impossible task. The examination would have to wait until Max could be tranquilised.

The Kronovet veterinary clinic near Brasov was about to have a most unusual day. People were still bringing in their pets for treatment and the waiting room had a collection of people holding pet dogs, cats and even rabbits. But just before mid-day the British and Romanian eye specialists descended on the clinic and took over the main surgery room, which had to be adapted to take on a much larger animal than it was designed for.

The operating table which would normally be adequate for even the largest dog, was far too small for Max. David and his team worked miracles in re-designing the room. Three normal tables were strapped together and the anaesthetic machine was modified to cope with a larger animal. By the time the sanctuary team arrived with Max, the veterinary clinic had become a magnet for local journalists who had heard about this unique operation and were keen to report on the story. Not only was this the first ever eye operation undertaken on a bear in Romania but Max was a well known bear due to his constant presence on the streets over the past decade.

Trying to save Max's sight

Max is taken to the veterinary surgery in Brasov for assessment of his eye injuries. Romanian journalists reported the story and Max became a celebrity!

Max has to be tranquilised so that David and Claudia can examine him.

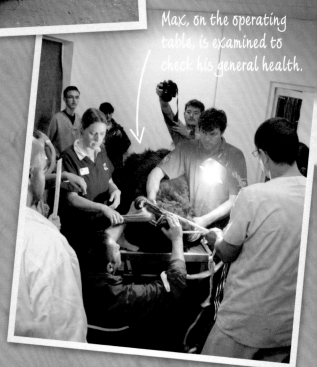

Max, on the operating table, is examined to check his general health.

David and Claudia test Max's eyes to see if his sight can be saved. The news is not good – detached retinas mean he will never be able to see.

The following day, Max is taken to his own enclosed area of the forest sanctuary complete with pool, trees and den.

He takes his first cautious steps of his new life . . .

. . . and here he is enjoying his first winter at the sanctuary, a far cry from chains and railings.

The staff would ensure he could spend the rest of his life in the forest.

The bear was tranquilised and brought into the operating room on a large stretcher, past the amazed pet owners holding tightly on to their dogs and cats. It took 6 people to lift the 250 kilos of bear onto the table. Liz and her Romanian counterparts immediately ensured the bear was properly tranquilised and began monitoring his breathing and heartbeat.

David and Claudia wasted no time in preparing their specialist instruments to test Max's eyes. One test used ultrasound which showed exactly what the problem was with Max's eyesight and it was not good. Claudia explained, sadly, that both of the bear's eyes appeared to have detached retinas. It is possible that the bear had been born with this defect but detached retinas can also be the result of massive trauma to the head, such as heavy blows to the head of a young animal. There was nothing they could do to improve his eyesight.

Back in the waiting room Cristina was saddened to hear that Max would never be able to see properly. He would never be able to mix with the bears in the main forest sanctuary enclosure as it would be too much of a risk for him. Nevertheless, she saw the positive side and said she would ensure Max had the best life in a small forest area of his own.

The very next day Max was released into the forest sanctuary in an area next to the enclosure where Gina and Sophia had been living. Max's forest had a shallow water pool, a den where he could rest and even hibernate, and over an acre of trees and shrubs.

Although Max could not see his new home, he still had a good sense of touch, hearing and smell and those heightened senses would compensate for his loss of sight. It was an emotional day for the sanctuary staff. They had cared for this bear as best they could and now they would ensure he could spend the rest of his life out in the forest.

Max's first steps into the forest were slow and ponderous. He was unsure of the earth beneath his paws as it was soft and yielding, unlike the concrete pavement where he had spent most of his life. He walked unsteadily across the earth, smelling everything before him.

His legs were shaking, partly due to apprehension, but also due to lack of exercise while in captivity. He had only ever walked 10 metres twice a day, from his small cage to the railings by the roadside and back again. It must have been a frightening time for the anxious bear. He stumbled into trees and tripped over bushes and panicked a few times, rushing and tripping again, but after a short time he calmed down, settled next to a tree and slept.

Over the following days and weeks, Max slowly padded around the whole enclosure and got used to his new home. He now even enjoys a bath in the large pool and he spent his first winter hibernating in his own den in the forest. Cristina is overjoyed to watch the steady progress of this once mistreated bear and every now and then Romanian journalists still report on how the famous bear is getting on.

Miro, the bear cub

MIRO WAS THE FIRST BABY BEAR BROUGHT to the sanctuary, in May 2007. He had been born around January or February of that year. Brown bears living in countries with cold winters, such as Romania, give birth to their young in hibernation dens in the winter period, usually around December or January.

Miro had been found by someone walking in the forests around the Persani Mountains, 80 km north of Brasov. It is likely that the cub's mother had been killed by hunters. But at least someone had brought the cub to the sanctuary and this was actually a great achievement for the project. In the past, any cub found in the forest had ended up either in a zoo or more likely in a cage in someone's garden where it would have been kept as a pet, until it grew out of its cuddly stage, and then would have been neglected and left to live a miserable life in its cramped cage.

Miro's arrival at the sanctuary caused quite a stir as everyone wanted to come and see the new cub, but it also caused a few problems. The sanctuary had been set up to provide a retirement home for rescued bears which had spent years in roadside cages or poor zoos. Looking after a baby bear was going to take a lot of extra work.

Emi and Lotzi had the task of trying to care for the cub and had to learn fast what food to give him, how to handle him, and more importantly where to put the little animal. When he was brought in he was like a furious teddy bear, wanting to rush around and play with people, but his play was quite rough. Even at such a young age he had sharp teeth and claws. In the wild, he would have had his mother and possibly another sibling to play with and his early life would have revolved around play, through which he would learn to fend for himself in the forest.

Emi had to take on the role of playmate and mother to the cub. He was about 5 months old and still needed to be fed on milk, but not just normal cow's milk. The milk needed to have vitamin supplements, so milk powder normally used for human babies was given to him.

It would be a month or two before he would start to eat solid food such as fruits, so Emi sat patiently and fed him milk through a bottle several times a day. Miro enjoyed this time as he would alternately feed then try to wrestle with Emi's arms or legs, and she ended up with plenty of scratches. But she also loved the cub and learned a lot from observing him and caring for him.

At first, Miro was kept in a caged area of the quarantine site but, as soon as he had been weaned off milk and was eating solid food, Lotzi wanted to get the cub out into a forest enclosure to let the young animal have the freedom to run and climb trees. He built a small fenced area which contained a few trees, a den to sleep in and a fresh water pool. It was next to the larger forest enclosure of Gina and Sophia so Miro would also be able to see and smell the older bears nearby.

Paul Hammond came to advise them on how to make the enclosure bear cub-proof, as cubs climb very easily and very quickly, so the fenced perimeter had to be designed carefully. On the inside of the main forest enclosures there is a series of electric wires which prevent the bears from climbing. They touch the fence with their nose and get a shock which teaches them to keep away from it. But Paul didn't want to put electric wires in the cub's enclosure, so another method was used. A sheet of metal over a metre high was put around the inside of the fence, a metre up from the ground. This meant that Miro could not get a grip on the metal and he couldn't climb it. So it was escape proof, even for an escape artist such as an energetic bear cub.

Miro showed all the characteristics of a young cub. In the wild he would have stayed with his mother for 2 years before venturing out on his own. During that time he would have felt secure with his mother and she would have shown him where to find the best foods in the forest, while protecting him from other bears. Normally a female brown bear gives birth to two or three cubs, sometimes four, and having siblings for company really helps a bear cub develop its natural behaviour. Cubs need to spend time playing, play fighting and preparing for life on their own. Bears are solitary animals once they leave their mother's side but they need to know how to interact with any bears they come across, so their play and their interactions with mother and siblings are essential preparation for adult life.

Without his mother for comfort or another cub to share his play, Miro was a sad young bear and spent a lot of time wailing. When he wasn't crying, he would be furiously sucking his paw while making a humming sound.

Miro needed the company of another cub on which to vent his energy in play, but on his own, he vented his frustration on his paw.

This behaviour stopped when someone was near him but as soon as he was left on his own, the pitiful cries and humming would echo throughout the sanctuary forest. It was a tough time for the workers at the sanctuary, but this is typical behaviour of a bear cub taken from its mother too young.

This is how hundreds of bear cubs spend their time in the horrendous Bear Parks in Japan. These Parks are simply zoos where large numbers of bears are kept in barren, featureless concrete pits for the entertainment of visitors. They are much like the Bear Pits of mediaeval Europe. Many badly managed zoos around the world also keep solitary cubs in cages and the result is usually a very sad bear cub, crying and sucking on its paw, much as a human child would suck on its thumb for comfort.

WSPA gave Cristina a report written by Sally Maughan, who runs the Idaho Black Bear Rehabilitation Centre, in the USA. Sally's report was packed full of invaluable information on how to care for bear cubs, including feeding and understanding their behaviour. Sally has cared for orphaned bear cubs for more than twenty years and has looked after over 200 young bears. Most of these had been brought to her when they were only a few months old and she cared for them until they were a year to eighteen months of age, after which they would be taken back to the mountains and released, with a radio collar around their necks to allow the authorities to monitor their progress.

Ciprian, the bear sanctuary vet, noticed that Miro's constant sucking on his right paw had made it sore and it was starting to bleed, so he wanted to clean the wound to prevent possible infection. While Lotzi tried to hold the little cub still, Ciprian began to cut away the fur on his paw. Miro didn't like being held still and squirmed to get free but Cristina tempted the cub with honey and he eagerly lapped up the sweet syrup, giving Ciprian enough time to spray the wounded paw with disinfectant. But as soon as the cub was released, Miro sucked his paw again. But at least it had been cleaned, and the cub never suffered from any infections.

There was nothing to be done to cure the cub's behaviour. He would grow out of it in a few months time, as all cubs do. If only Miro had another cub to play with. He needed the company of another cub on which to vent his energy in play but, on his own, he vented his frustration on his paw.

Bear cubs grow quickly, and Miro's behaviour changed dramatically over the next few months and he calmed down. At least he had Gina and Sophia in the enclosure next to his and he could see and smell them as they raced around in their own patch of forest.

Cristina wanted to put Miro in with the sisters but they were a year older than him and, at under a year old, Miro was too small to risk putting them together. The following year when he was around 18 months old he was allowed to join Gina and Sophia. He had grown quite a bit in size but was still smaller than the other two juvenile bears who were two and a half years old by then. Yet he was big enough to play with them and seemed to enjoy taunting the sisters by jumping out on them when they were relaxing by the pool and then racing away as fast as possible when they became fed up of his pestering.

Gina and Sophia were later moved into the large forest enclosure with the adult bears. By then more young cubs had been brought to the sanctuary to join Miro but it would not be long before Miro would be big enough to live with the adult bears and he wouldn't ever be lonely again.

below: Miro having fun in the snow.

Rescues put on hold

THE RESCUE OF BEARS WAS GOING AHEAD faster than anticipated. By mid 2007 there were 30 bears at the sanctuary, some already in the forest enclosures and others lined up in quarantine areas, being prepared for release into the forest. Then a disastrous turn of events put all the rescue work on hold.

There are thousands of bears living peacefully in the forests of Romania but when people build hotels, houses, towns and farms right next to the bears' habitat it is inevitable that some wild bears will come into conflict with people. Although it is rare for bears to attack people, there have been a few serious interac-

tions between people and bears in Romania in recent years.

There had been a couple of human fatalities due to bear encounters around Brasov during 2005 and 2006 and, in late 2007, a bear had been seen feeding at night in gardens and farm areas a few miles away from Zarnesti, where the bear sanctuary was situated.

The local people had tried to scare the bear away on several occasions, once reportedly attacking the bear with a pitchfork, but this had resulted in a villager being mauled by the injured bear. Hunters were then brought in to track the bear down and a few days later it was shot.

right: CCTV cameras were erected and cover all areas of the sanctuary.
opposite page: Tree collars are placed around the trunks of trees near the perimeter to prevent bears climbing them.

There are many bears living in the forests around Brasov and Zarnesti but most of the time they are secretive and rarely seen. However, when there is an incident like this, no matter how rare it may be, the local community can become nervous and seek action to prevent any further incidents.

Having shot the wild bear, the local authorities decided to check the bear sanctuary at Zarnesti, to allay any concern that bears could escape to cause problems for farmers and people living in the forest areas.

A delegation of people, including representatives from the Hunting Association, the mayor's office, Environment Guards and the Forestry Department came to inspect the sanctuary. Although they were impressed with the safety of the enclosures and the electric fencing, they made a report outlining a variety of concerns which had to be addressed before any further bears could be moved into the sanctuary forest enclosures.

The main security concerns centred on a number of trees that were close to the inside of the sanctuary fence. These trees were already surrounded by electric wires to prevent any bear attempting to climb up and somehow drop over the fence to escape. But they wanted all trees within 5 metres of the fence to be chopped down as a safety precaution.

Another issue was monitoring the bears within the sanctuary. They wanted to be sure that all the bears could be checked regularly and one option was to have all the bears fitted with some form of micro-chip or neck collar that would emit a signal showing exactly where the bear was at all times.

These were difficult issues to resolve. Roger Lapis was insistent that no more trees should be cut down as he wanted to protect the natural forest as much as possible for the bears within, so another way had to be found to ensure the trees were impossible to climb.

As for the tracking of the bears, there were new micro-chip ear tags coming onto the market that were being used to track farm animals from a hundred metres, and these were also currently being tested on wild bears such as polar bears to monitor their movements over a restricted area. But these high-tech tracking devices were expensive and as yet unproven for use over long

left: Roger checking the CCTV in the sanctuary control room.
opposite page: A view through the sanctuary showing the tree collars in place along the perimeter fence.

periods. It would also mean a lot of stress to those bears who had already been released in the forest sanctuary as they would have to be tranquilised in the large forest enclosures to bring them out again to fit the ear tags.

But these issues now had to be resolved as the authorities insisted no further bear rescues could be undertaken until the extra security measures at the sanctuary were in place.

As the late autumn was drawing in and winter weather was only a few months away it looked unlikely that any more bears could be rescued for some time and those bears already in quarantine areas had to stay there for the foreseeable future.

While investigations were being made into which method of tracking the bears in the enclosure could be used, Roger set about planning how to save the trees. One option was to move the perimeter fence further outwards, away from the trees, but that would be difficult, time consuming and expensive.

The solution came in the form of an umbrella, a tree umbrella. To make sure that the trees near the perimeter fence were totally un-climbable by the bears, a metal umbrella-like collar was designed and fastened two metres up around the trunk of each of the selected trees.

The electric wires around the base of the tree already prevented any bear from attempting to climb the tree, but the new collars made it impossible for them to do so and therefore prevented the need to cut the trees down. Roger and Cristina were delighted and they set to work building the collars and fixing them to the few trees that had been selected as being close to the fence.

The monitoring of the bears within the enclosures took more time. The micro-chip and ear tag devices were not going to work well within a forest environment so another solution had to be found. It was decided that a CCTV camera system had to be installed along the whole perimeter fence which would enable sanctuary security guards to see what the bears were doing at all hours of the day and night and also, very importantly, it would serve as a security system to prevent any human intruders coming close to the sanctuary.

But all of this extra work took months to

complete. Cristina went to the Romanian Ministry of Environment in Bucharest to plead with the Minister to allow her to rescue more bears or at least to move the bears from quarantine into the forest enclosures. But although sympathetic to the project, the Minister would not agree to lift the ban on bear movements until all the security work had been completed and approved.

The CCTV cameras were fitted, computers and monitors were set up in the sanctuary's main building and a 24 hour security guard system was installed to monitor the cameras.

The main security concerns centred on a number of trees that were close to the inside of the sanctuary fence.

Tree collars were fitted. Parts of the fence were strengthened and the electric fence was checked and double checked but, by the time all this had been completed, the winter weather had arrived and work once again came to a halt.

Many bears hibernated in the forest or in the quarantine dens over winter but a few remained awake and seemed to enjoy playing in the deep snow and skidding over the iced up ponds. The sanctuary workers continued to deliver food to these bears and worked tirelessly, driving through the thick snow on the mountain road each day to ensure they could check on the bears.

Wild bears were known to pass through the forest above Zarnesti where the bear sanctuary was located. Bear paw prints were frequently seen in the mud and snow, sometimes showing bears had walked around the sanctuary perimeter fence before moving on. For that reason the sanctuary fences also have an electric wire on the outside, to deter wild animals such as bears, wild pigs, deer and even people, from approaching the fence too closely.

2008 – Second forest enclosure

WHEN THE SNOW FINALLY GAVE WAY TO spring showers and sunshine during March of 2008, the local authorities came to check the security improvements at the sanctuary and finally gave their approval. Bear rescue work could start again.

Thirty bears had already been rescued and most were now living in the forest enclosures while some had overwintered and hibernated in the quarantine dens. A second large enclosure was needed to ensure the remaining bears could be accommodated. More zoos were closing down and the bears from those zoos were added to the list to be rescued by the bear sanctuary.

Funds were raised to finance the construction work and over the winter period the fence had started to go up, two large fresh water pools were dug out and a number of hibernation dens were built. CCTV cameras were installed around the fence and this time no tree-umbrellas were needed as the new fence had

left: Lydia explores her new home.
below: Inspecting the new enclosure.

been positioned a few metres distant from trees. By April 2008 the work was finished and the large 8 hectare forest enclosure was ready for its first occupants.

The first bears to be moved into this second enclosure were Lydia and Cristi. When they were rescued from cages behind a destroyed restaurant in 2005, a small forest enclosure had been built in the sanctuary just for them. Now that a new large enclosure was ready, it was a good time to give these two bears a further taste of freedom and let them mix and interact with other rescued bears.

The best plan (plan A) was to entice the bears one by one into a transport cage and move them the 200 metres along the sanctuary road to their new large forest home. But bears are intelligent animals and they don't always do what is expected of them.

Lotzi took a large transport cage into Lydia and Cristi's enclosure, baited it with sugary food and set the open door on a trip wire which could be controlled from outside of the enclosure. Meanwhile, Emi had been at the far end of the enclosure talking to the bears through the fence and feeding them titbits to keep them occupied.

With the trap set, Lotzi sat outside the enclosure with a rope to the cage door in his grip, waiting for the bears to take the bait. Emi now returned to the front of the enclosure and called to the bears, who dutifully ambled over to see if more food was on offer.

The cage presented both bears with an unexpected intrusion into their territory and they eyed it with great suspicion. But the sight and smell of food inside, was tempting. Both bears seemed very wary of the open door and despite the closeness of the food, they would not enter the cage. Cristi tried digging underneath the cage seemingly believing he could get at the

food from under the cage. After two hours of this, the sanctuary team decided to resort to plan B, which was to tranquilise the bears and carry them to their new forest enclosure.

Paul Hammond was there to supervise and he loaded the dart gun and waited for Lydia to sit near the fence. She was likely to be the more nervous bear so she would be moved first. Paul's aim was good. The crack of the gun and the shock of the tranquiliser dart hitting her in her thigh made Lydia race away into the forest, closely followed by Cristi, who was spooked by her reaction.

After a 15 minute wait, Lotzi and Paul drove into the enclosure in the JCB vehicle, picked up the cage and took it to where Lydia was now sleeping soundly in a patch of open grass. Cristi stayed far away from the noise of the JCB, so the team quickly checked Lydia was fully tranquilised and hauled her into the cage, lifted it onto the JCB and carried her out of the enclosure.

The cage containing the sleeping and snoring bear was positioned next to the gate leading into the new large forest enclosure but Lydia was still fast asleep and had to be left a couple of hours to come round. When she eventually

awoke, the cage and enclosure gate were both opened allowing Lydia to step out into the forest. She peered out into the new area and spent some time pacing up and down in the cage before making a run out into the forest. She ran down a slope leading to the newly constructed water pool where she stopped and sat drinking water before heading off at a more leisurely pace to explore the rest of her new home. There were no other bears in the enclosure yet so Lydia was able to explore without any confrontations. Cristi was enticed into the transport cage with food the next day and he became the second bear released into the new 8 hectare forest area.

Cristi has put on weight and appears happy to wander round the forest, stretching up against a tree to scratch his huge back, but his favourite pastime in the heat of summer is to sit in the large water pool, cooling off and playing with the sticks floating around, while Lydia fusses around the trees always searching for another morsel of food. They had spent many years together confined in a small barren cage where their tempers were often frayed, but in the forest they clearly seem to be best of friends and are never far from each other. Often Cristi will amble over to Lydia and lean his massive head on her shoulder. The years of deprivation in the mini-zoo cages are a distant memory to these bears who now appear to be relaxed and enjoying their stress-free lives in the forest sanctuary.

Martinica, the Monastery bear

ONE OF THE REMARKABLE DEVELOPMENTS in the campaign to rescue bears from illegal captivity in Romania was the strength of public support for this work. Every step along the way to creating the bear sanctuary was supported by the public. The Mayor of Zarnesti had agreed to provide the 69 hectares of forest for the sanctuary and, as the building got under way and bears began to be rescued and moved to the sanctuary, the Romanian media also gave the campaign its full support.

The Romanian media endorsement of the project was largely a result of the hard work undertaken by Cristina Lapis, who was such a good ambassador for animals that the media turned to her whenever there was an issue of animal welfare in the news. She appeared on innumerable TV news items, on chat shows, in newspaper articles and radio interviews. Although her work to help the stray dogs of Romania was well known, she quickly became a powerful spokesperson for the bears.

Whenever a new bear was brought to the sanctuary or when anything of interest was happening with the rescued bears, the Romanian TV and journalists would turn up to cover the story.

One of Romania's radio stations, called Hot-News, gave its full support to the rescue of captive bears. They started a page on their web site asking for anyone who had news of a captive bear to send them the details and location. A stream of people responded, explaining where they had seen caged bears. Many of these bears were already known to the bear sanctuary team but there were still a few surprises.

In 2008 a few people had written in to say that a 5 year old male bear was being kept in a cage at the famous fourteenth-century Cotmeana Monastery, a few hundred kilometres north of Bucharest. A Romanian TV crew went to film the bear, called Martinica, and found that the Patriarch of the Monastery was not prepared to give up his 'pet' bear.

HotNews then started an on-line petition to save the bear. Over 3,000 signatures were sent to the Minister for Environment urging him to ensure the bear was legally confiscated and re-homed in the forest sanctuary at Zarnesti.

below: Martinica is rescued from his old cage.

Martinica was not impressed by the outside world. It took a week before he was comfortable with the forest experience.

In October 2008 the Patriarch relented and, with the help of the National Environment Guard, the bear sanctuary team rescued the starving Martinica from his cage and took him to the sanctuary.

Before Martinica could be released into the sanctuary forest enclosure, he had to undergo a surgical castration. This is to ensure there is no breeding in the sanctuary. If the bears were free to breed, it would soon cause a population explosion, filling the sanctuary with cubs, so the policy is to surgically castrate all male bears that have to stay in the sanctuary for life. It is, after all, a retirement home for rescued bears, and space is limited.

The operation was undertaken by Liviu Harbuz, who is the Chief Veterinary Advisor to the bear sanctuary. Liviu was also the President of the Veterinarians' College of Romania and in 2009 he was the State Secretary of the Romanian government's Ministry of Agriculture. The castration operation is quite straightforward and takes around 30 minutes to complete, but as Martinica had become such a famous bear in the eyes of the Romanian media, the day of the operation saw a dozen television and newspaper crews descend on the sanctuary to record the event.

Liviu and his team were filmed tranquilising the bear and preparing him for the operation. The media crews then respectfully kept their distance once the operation was underway. Several Romanian TV programmes broadcast the

operation that evening and local newspapers featured the story the following day. The general media and public view was one of pride in the bear sanctuary and all aspects of its work.

Martinica was allowed to recover from his ordeal in the comfort of the large quarantine dens located in the main building. These dens all have outside access into a small area of forest known as the 'training area'. This is usually the first taste the rescued bears have of the forest and of the sanctuary fence and, as each bear's reactions can differ, it is best that they are first introduced to this small area of forest with no other bears around as they can then retreat back into the quarantine den for comfort if needed.

It is important that the bears learn quickly and safely about the forest enclosure and about the electric fence surrounding it. All bears need to touch the fence at least once so that they learn that it is something to avoid in future. The electric shock doesn't physically harm the animals but it is a sharp sting which the bear would prefer not to repeat.

Anyone who has accidentally touched an electrified cattle fence and has received a powerful jolt quickly learns to keep away in future. In addition to the 8 electric wires running the height of the inside of the fence, there is also 1 electric wire on the outside of the enclosure fence which is meant to deter wild pigs, deer, dogs and even wild bear from getting close to the enclosure. The efficiency of this system has been clearly shown on numerous occasions when cameramen filming the bears through the fence have accidentally touched the wire. Their initial shriek, followed by a burst of swearing demonstrates the effectiveness of the fence!

Martinica spent a few days in the den recovering from his operation before the door leading from the den into the forest training area was opened. But Martinica was not impressed by the outside world with its strange trees and spongy earth. For the first day he sat with just his head peering out of the den. He was afraid to step out of his comfortable lair into the unknown. He played with stones and sticks within paw's reach of the den and seemed content to rest there all day.

It took a week before he was comfortable with the forest experience. On his first short venture out of the den, he touched the electric fence, got a shock on his nose, raced back inside the den and stayed there. But he eventually overcame his fear as the sights and smells of the forest enticed him back into the natural habitat. Before long he was enjoying the large forest enclosure, the pools, trees and the variety of forest food.

Martinica was initially a little nervous of other bears. He had spent all his life in a cage in the centre of a quiet Monastery with only the coming and going of monks, feeding him scraps of food. As with the other rescued bears, time will heal his fears and the forest sights and smells will eventually help him get used to being a bear again.

Bears on TV

THE BEAR SANCTUARY WAS GETTING A LOT of media attention. Romanian TV, radio and newspapers loved the project and featured updates whenever a new bear was rescued. There was also media interest from abroad and TV crews had filmed there for programmes such as the BBC's *Countryfile*, a Dutch Children's TV programme and numerous German news stories.

In May of 2008, the Australian TV 'Channel 10' sent a crew to Romania to make a TV documentary on the bear sanctuary. They brought with them Natalie Imbruglia, a well known Australian pop singer and actress. Natalie was to be the presenter of the TV documentary and would spend a week at the sanctuary and travelling with the sanctuary team rescuing bears.

Natalie had heard all about the old Asiatic black bear called Ursula who was still living in the decaying Buhusi Zoo and during her visit she was able to see Ursula rescued and brought to the sanctuary.

When the sanctuary team arrived at Buhusi Zoo to rescue Ursula, she was easily tempted out of her confined zoo cage with pieces of fresh apple and bread with honey. Once in the sanctuary transport cage it was easier to inspect her. She seemed in reasonable health for her age which, at around 26 years, meant she was quite elderly. In the wild she would probably have reached an age of 15 to 20 years but in captivity these hardy animals can live to over 35 years. However, her eyesight was badly affected. She had an opaque cataract covering the iris of her left eye and the beginnings of a cataract on her right eye, which meant she would be partially blind. It is likely that the cataracts had developed due to vitamin deficiency in her diet. Similar cataracts have been seen in bears kept on a bread and water diet for life, as dancing bears in Turkey.

With the support of a local Romanian group called the 'Lions Roar', Cristina was able to build a small forest enclosure just for Ursula. As an old and partially blind bear of a different species to the brown bears in the sanctuary, it was important to allow Ursula the privacy to live out her remaining years in peace within her own patch of natural forest. She took some time to settle down in the

opposite page: Ursula in her decaying cage at the Buhusi Zoo where she lived for over 20 years.
left: Rescue by the bear sanctuary team.
above and below: Ursula amongst the vegetation at the sanctuary.

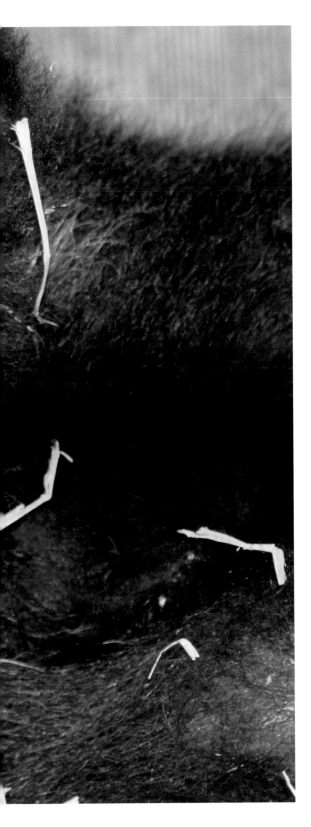

enclosure as her blindness meant she spent the first week bumping into trees but, little by little, she learned how to get around her new home and soon seemed content to spend her days sleeping in the sunshine on the grass and earth of the Zarnesti bear sanctuary or bathing in the fresh water pool. Hopefully, she will have quite a few more years left to enjoy the natural surroundings that were forbidden to her for most of her life.

Natalie was delighted to have been able to see Ursula given a new life at the sanctuary. In addition to seeing one of the sanctuary's oldest residents, Natalie was lucky to have been visiting the sanctuary just after its youngest resident was brought in.

RUDI

Rudi was a four month old brown bear cub who had been found wandering near a hospital on the outskirts of Brasov. Brasov is surrounded by the forests of the Carpathian Mountains and many brown bears live in close proximity to the city. Some bears wander into public areas to search for food in rubbish bins. Rudi's mother had probably come out of the forests in search of food and somehow had become parted from her cub.

Luckily for Rudi, the bear sanctuary had been well publicised in the Romanian media so the people who found the helpless animal took him straight to the sanctuary.

At just a few months of age, Rudi was a

living teddy bear, cute and playful and a bundle of energy. He craved attention and it was down to Emi to care for him. As a very young cub, Rudi needed bottle feeding several times a day and whenever he was left in his quarantine den, he would wail for attention.

In between bottle feeding him, Emi let him run around the grassy slopes on the edge of the sanctuary. He had a warm straw-filled den near the quarantine area but like all young cubs he needed a lot of attention and really needed his mother and siblings to play with.

When Emi left him in his den to go about her other work, the cub would wail pitifully as she walked away. The cries of a young cub are loud and sound similar to those of a human baby. As difficult as it might be to ignore a baby bear

crying out for attention, Emi knew from caring for Miro the previous year that, however hard she tried to mother the cub, she could never be with him 24 hours a day and that was what he needed. When she let the cub run around outside, he would never stray far from where she sat patiently watching him. Now and then, he would race back and grab hold of her leg or arm in his strong paws and give a fierce nip which she could feel even through thick jeans.

Natalie was captivated by the young cub and she could appreciate how someone might want to keep such a cute animal as a pet. But bear cubs grow quickly and within 6 months Rudi would be a large adolescent bear, capable of seriously injuring someone with his super-sharp teeth and claws.

At least for a few weeks Rudi was allowed to run around in the grass under the careful eye of Emi. Soon, however, he would be placed into a forest enclosure to learn about trees and water pools and about other bears.

The bear sanctuary had been set up to care for rescued captive bears which were unable to be returned to the wild. The sanctuary did not yet have the specialist knowledge to support a bear cub rehabilitation programme which could care for and release young bears back into the wild. There was a small project already doing some work to release orphaned bear cubs in the north of Romania and the sanctuary staff aimed to liaise with them at a later date.

Natalie Imbruglia was hugely impressed

with the bear sanctuary and its dedicated staff. Her documentary was later shown on TV in Australia and New Zealand and brought more public interest and support for the ongoing work of rescuing and caring for bears in Romania.

DIANA

A couple of months after Rudi was rescued, the sanctuary received a call from a family living in a small village in the west of Romania. They had a young bear which they were keeping as a pet but the 'pet' was running riot in their house. Could the sanctuary find a home for her?

On arrival at the village, the sanctuary team were faced by a surprising situation. The family said they had 'found' the bear in the forest nearby when it was just a few weeks old and its eyes were not even open. They felt sorry for the cub and kept her as a pet. Diana, as they had named her, had spent the last 6 months living with the family, eating scraps from their meals and she even slept in the same bed as the old grandmother and had her own pillow!

The family clearly loved the young bear but, at 6 months of age, the cub was rapidly turning from a cuddly pet into a destructive terror. The cute 'teddy-bear' phase only lasts a few months and by 6 months of age a bear cub will have grown larger than a pet dog, with claws and teeth much sharper and longer.

The cub still had the run of the house and front yard but, from the scratches covering the arms and legs of the family members, especially the granny, it was clear they could no longer cope with a growing bear in their home.

The young bear had been well fed on kitchen scraps and was in good health. Lotzi sat down with the family and explained that it was illegal to keep a wild bear and that in future anyone finding a cub should alert the sanctuary immediately. He tried to entice Diana into the transport cage but the cub would have none of it. Sensing that her freedom to run riot in the household was about to end, she rushed for the garden gate and escaped out into the dusty streets of the quiet village.

Lotzi raced after her and a few minutes later returned with a struggling, kicking and biting Diana in his strong grip. With tears in their eyes the whole family waved from their front gate as Diana, now safely caged in the back of the sanctuary van, turned down the street and out of the village on her way to Zarnesti.

Three hours later, Rudi was to get the shock of his short life as Diana was put into the same large caged den that he had occupied on his own for the past couple of months. Although they were the same age, having been born around January that year, Diana was larger than Rudi, probably because of the food lavished on her by her human family. She confidently entered the den with no hesitation while Rudi scampered up the walls of the den in pure terror at another young animal being so close.

Later that day Rudi was still high up in the den while Diana ambled around as if she couldn't care less about the other young bear. Lotzi couldn't help laughing as he tried to coax

Rudi down to meet his new playmate. But a few days later the two bears began to play together and the cubs took comfort from each other. These two cubs would stay in the dens until the following year when they would be big enough to be put into a small forest enclosure of their own.

Another media success for the sanctuary was to have a TV series made about it and shown on the Animal Planet TV channel. Over a period of 18 months during 2007 and 2008, a professional TV production company from the UK, called Imago, filmed at various times of the year and made a series of 7 half-hour programmes following the daily work at the bear sanctuary.

They filmed bears being rescued from zoos, restaurants and houses as well as the veterinary work and operations undertaken on a number of bears and the release of the bears into the forest enclosures.

The TV crew was headed by Executive Producer Vivica Parsons and filming consultant Graham Creelman. Imago had an excellent track record of producing TV documentaries on animal issues and had made several films highlighting bear and orang-utan protection projects in previous years with the WSPA.

Vivica and Graham were thoroughly supportive of the work being done to create the bear sanctuary in Romania and all filming was undertaken with the welfare of the animals as a priority.

In contrast to this, some film crews do not understand, or in some cases do not care, about the affect their actions might have on the animals they are filming. Too often a film crew will want too much, too quickly, in order to get their story. However, when filming animals, a good camera crew not only needs patience but also a good understanding of the nature of the animals they are focusing on.

With the rescue of a bear from a cage in a zoo there are no second takes. If the bear suddenly shows signs of moving into the transport cage after 2 hours of hiding in a corner, the action of trapping the bear in the cage can take seconds and, if the cameraman has not assessed the situation correctly, he may miss the vital point of the rescue. The bear cannot be asked to do it all over again!

Similarly with filming the bears in the forest enclosures, it is only with patience and a knowledge of the bears' natural behaviour that the cameraman can capture remarkable film of bears quietly doing their own thing. The Imago

above and opposite: Vivica Parsons, Graham Creelman and crew of Imago Productions filming the *Bear Sanctuary* TV series for Animal Planet.

cameramen took wonderful film of the bears playing in the water pools, play-fighting in the open meadows, reaching up and scratching their backs on a tree trunk and feeding leisurely off the vegetation in the sanctuary enclosures.

The Imago team worked professionally and the programme they produced, called appropriately *Bear Sanctuary*, was well received and is expected to be repeated on the Animal Planet TV channel over the coming years. The series was also shown on Romanian TV and has helped gain more local followers of the sanctuary project as well as creating more awareness about the need to protect these animals in the wild.

A few more bears were brought to the sanctuary during the late autumn of 2008. One was a young female cub who had been found in the forest with her leg caught in a trap. She was brought to the bear sanctuary in a pitiful condition, weighing only 15 kilos. As the veterinary expertise necessary to help the cub was not available in Brasov, she was sent to the University Veterinary Hospital in Bucharest where she was operated on by Dr. Liviu Harbuz, who is the most experienced wildlife vet in Romania.

The cub, later named Cleo, needed several operations to save her back leg but after months of recovery she was eventually well enough to be released into a small forest enclosure at the bear sanctuary with a few other young bears. Today Cleo still walks with a limp due to a shortening of her leg bones, but she is able to run and climbs trees as well as any other bear.

By the winter of 2008 there were 40 rescued bears living at the Zarnesti bear sanctuary. A heavy winter snow encouraged these bears to hibernate until the following spring.

Snow bears

Not all of the bears hibernate during the winter, some of them just want to play in the snow!

Still friends!

Chilling out . . .

Taking a leisurely walk
in the snow-covered
sanctuary.

2009 – Bear serenade

THE NEW YEAR OF 2009 STARTED QUIETLY at the bear sanctuary. Many bears slept for several months but a few stayed awake to enjoy the snow. The sanctuary staff continued their constant maintenance of the enclosures and waited for the weather to improve so they could resume rescuing bears.

In early spring, three bears were rescued from an old zoo which had been unable to feed them. They were in a very poor condition with ragged coats and very thin bodies. If they had been left another month they may not have survived. At the sanctuary they were given a warm

quarantine den and plenty of food and water. Within a few months of their rescue their health had improved dramatically and they had put on tens of kilos of weight. They were unrecognisable as the poor animals brought from the zoo on the verge of death.

In early summer of 2009 the sanctuary received information that a caged bear was being kept in a garden of a house in the middle of Bucharest, Romania's capital city. Cristina Lapis liaised with the relevant authorities to get the necessary paperwork to legally confiscate the bear and the sanctuary team set off before dawn to travel to the capital city, 170 km south of Zarnesti.

The van containing the transport cage was parked in the alleyway leading to the garden where the bear was kept in a cage. An officer from the Ministry of Environment was there, accompanied by police, to issue the legal paperwork for confiscating the bear. As usual, the story had got round the news agencies and several TV news crews and journalists had arrived early to report on the bear rescue.

But the owner of the bear did not want to co-operate. He refused to let the Ministry man into his house to inspect the bear. It took a couple of hours of tense negotiations with the police before the bear could be taken. Finally, the owner brought an 18 month old male bear out into the street, controlling him by a rope around his neck. The young bear was clearly frightened but the owner wanted to tell his

above: Fiona Pears plays for Max.
opposite page: A bear is rescued from a house in Bucharest.

story to the waiting journalists, claiming the police were taking away his well-loved pet.

He then showed the TV crews photos of him and his wife working with bears in a Romanian circus. It turned out that he had been a circus animal trainer and was proud of the fact that he had trained many bears to perform in local circuses. He then admitted that he also had 3 young 6 month old cubs in his house. These would have been illegally obtained, either bought from a zoo or taken from the wild. All 4 bears were put into the sanctuary vehicles and taken back to Zarnesti. The cubs would be sent to a rehabilitation project in the far north of the country but the 18 month old bear, called Dandy, would be released into the sanctuary forest area later in the year.

In September 2009 the sanctuary had a musical visitor. Fiona Pears is an internationally renowned violinist from New Zealand. Being a supporter of the WSPA, she had heard so much about the bear sanctuary that she wanted to visit and to play her violin to the bears. She wanted to know if her music would have any effect on the animals, especially on Max, the blind bear.

Fiona toured the sanctuary in fascination of the bears, many of which stopped to listen when she played her violin. Max came across to be near the fence where Fiona was playing and he sat for a few minutes listening. Fiona made a film of her visit to the sanctuary and added it to her next promotional DVD which she called *Bear Serenade* to encourage her fans to support this and other animal protection projects.

Throughout 2009, more zoos were closing down and although the Zarnesti sanctuary had two large forest enclosures, Milioane de Prieteni decided that a third enclosure would eventually be needed to ensure all the additional bears needing rescue could be properly cared for.

A large 9 hectares area of forest next to the second enclosure was mapped out for future construction. If the third enclosure was built, the Zarnesti bear sanctuary would, in total, have around 27 hectares of forested enclosures to provide a natural forest home to rescued bears. 50 bears were living in the sanctuary by the beginning of 2010, but a further 15 bears were on the sanctuary's list to be rescued.

2010 – Overseas visitor

ALL OF THE BEARS BROUGHT TO THE ZARNESTI bear sanctuary had been rescued from zoos and cages in Romania. But in May 2010 the sanctuary had a visitor from another continent. Betsy, a 24 year old female European brown bear had been rescued from a small cage in the middle of Houston, Texas, USA. The Houston Society for the Prevention of Cruelty to Animals (HSPCA) had investigated reports of wild animals being kept on a farm and had found cages containing tigers, American black bears and Betsy – a European brown bear.

The animals were all in poor condition and were legally confiscated and taken back to the Houston SPCA's rescue centre. The tigers and American bears were found new homes in local zoos but there seemed to be no zoo space for an old brown bear.

Patti Mercer, the CEO of the Houston SPCA, asked Cristina Lapis if Betsy could be re-homed in the Romanian bear sanctuary as she was the same species as the bears in the sanctuary. Cristina agreed to take in the bear and, after all the legal paperwork was completed for the import permits, Betsy was flown to Europe in a large transport crate.

Despite Betsy's age, she did not appear stressed by the long journey and eagerly emerged from her travel crate into the sunshine of the bear sanctuary enclosure in May 2010. Two members of the HSPCA staff (Tara Yurkshat – Vice President of Animal Welfare,

above: Betsy had spent over 20 years in a small cage at a private zoo in Texas, USA before she was rescued.
opposite page: Betsy makes a bee-line for the fresh-water pool after her long flight.

and Meera Nanlal – Public Relations Manager) together with Dr. Maud Marin (vet from Houston zoo) accompanied the bear and were thrilled to see her take her first steps on European soil. Betsy made a bee-line for the water pool and splashed around in pleasure. She had come home.

above: Singer Leona Lewis visits the Romanian bear sanctuary.

Celebrity visit

T HE BEAR SANCTUARY IS BECOMING WELL known not only in Romania but around the world and in July 2010 a surprise visitor to the sanctuary created a stir in the international media. The British singer Leona Lewis was a keen supporter of animal protection work around the world and knew about the Romanian bear rescues. So she made time to visit the sanctuary in between her hectic schedule of concert tours in the UK and USA.

Leona was thrilled to see the bears she had heard so much about. She was able to spend a relaxing day in the peace and tranquillity of the Carpathian Mountains, watching the rescued bears stroll around in their forest paradise. Leona later described her visit to her fans through her international web site, which was a great way to show her support and to create further public awareness of the need to protect the world's wildlife.

Zoo closure

WHAT STARTED AS A REASONABLY QUIET year ended up being very busy. In late October 2010 Cristina received the message from the Ministry of Environment that she had long been waiting for. They had prepared the legal paperwork to confiscate a 10 year old male bear called Muki.

Muki, had been caught from the wild as a cub and had lived for 10 years in a concrete and iron bar cage behind a hotel in the forest of Balvanyos, 80 km north of Brasov. Muki was treated as a local attraction, with people coming to the hotel restaurant to see the bear and feed him scraps of food from their meals. The owner said he loved the bear and everyone working at the restaurant believed the bear had a good life as he had all the food he needed.

below: Muki in the concrete and iron cage behind the hotel.

All that remained were three adult bears and a young wolf, and these animals would be euthanized if they were not re-homed.

But Muki did not have a good life. He had plenty of food, too much in fact, but confined to a cage with nothing to do all day except eat is no life for an adult male brown bear, and Muki became overweight. When finally rescued he weighed over 350 kilos, and could only plod around his cage waiting for the next meal. Adult male brown bears living in the forests of Romania would normally weigh around 200 kilos.

Cristina Lapis had heard about Muki several years previously, but initial attempts to legally confiscate the bear had failed as his owner claimed he was building a larger cage for him. He then said he would apply for a zoo licence so he could keep the bear in a mini-zoo behind the restaurant.

The local mayor also tried to prevent the bear being taken from the restaurant as Muki had been a popular tourist attraction for the Balvanyos region. But the attitude of the Romanian public towards this sort of spectacle had changed over the past few years, due to the work of the Zarnesti bear sanctuary.

As soon as Cristina had the news from the Ministry of Environment, her sanctuary team set off to the forests north of Brasov to recover the bear. On the day of the rescue Muki sat on the cold concrete floor of his cage waiting for his daily meal. Ciprian, the vet who has helped rescue most of the bears at the sanctuary, prepared his tranquiliser darts and fired through the rusty cage bars to sedate the bear. Once the bear was unconscious, it took 8 men to stretcher

the 350 kilos of sleeping bear up a muddy slope to the waiting vehicle.

Back at the sanctuary, Muki was released into a quarantine den which had access to the pool and trees of the forest training area. After a few days he emerged into this forest area with a bewildered look – not surprising as it was the first earth he had stepped on since his birth 10 years previously.

Just a few weeks later, Cristina had yet another emergency call. This time it was from the Municipality of Slatina, in the south of the country. Slatina Zoo was run-down and poorly managed. The local authorities claimed they could no longer afford to look after the animals and in the past year many of the animals had died. All that remained were three adult bears and a young wolf, and these animals would be euthanized if they were not re-homed, as the zoo was now about to be demolished.

Cristina would never consider leaving the animals to die but she was now running out of quarantine space at the sanctuary. Roger Lapis quickly arranged for new quarantine cages to be built which would give these new bears a warm place to hibernate over winter. This would give them time to regain their strength for when they were released into the forest enclosures. The starving wolf was also brought to the sanctuary and would later be released into an area of forest sanctuary.

Cristina said that the Slatina Zoo conditions were the worst she had ever seen. The bears

above: Muki looking out from his cage.

were starving and in a terrible condition with the zoo crumbling around them. The only positive thing was that many of these old-style zoos in Romania were now closing down forever.

As the winter weather enveloped the sanctuary in December 2010, 56 rescued bears slept safely within. Cristina and Roger Lapis and all the sanctuary staff were looking forward to a quieter period while the bears hibernated, but Cristina was well aware that there were still some bears suffering another winter in small, dirty cages in run-down zoos or in someone's back yard. So within a few months, the rescues would start again.

The sanctuary at work

THE FUTURE WORK OF THE ZARNESTI BEAR sanctuary is to continue to care for these rescued animals for the rest of their lives and to ensure that no more bears are kept in illegal captivity in Romania. The sanctuary also has an important role in creating positive public awareness for the protection of bears and other wildlife in Romania.

The sanctuary does not have the facilities to cater for individual visitors, but there are plans to allow organised tour groups to visit the sanctuary at set times of the day, hopefully from mid 2011. The visitors will be shown around the sanctuary by Mariana Bota, who is the education officer there.

Visitors will have to abide by the sanctuary rules. They have to respect the animals by not making a noise, not taking food or drink on the walk around the sanctuary, not smoking or dropping litter etc. Mariana often travels with the sanctuary team when a bear has to be confiscated so she knows the history of all the bears and she will explain the stories of the bears to the visitors.

Romanian school children are already visiting the sanctuary, under the guidance of Mariana, and teachers are keen to develop programs in the classroom to enhance the on-site experience with further lessons on the wildlife theme. In 2010 Cristina Lapis initiated a series of school programmes in Brasov and Zarnesti, to teach Romanian children about animal welfare and animal protection. Cristina aims to see these classes taken up by other schools throughout the country. In the future, the bear sanctuary hopes to develop an educational

above: Visitors to the sanctuary hoping for a glimpse of the bears.
opposite page: Mariana, the sanctuary education officer, and a group of school children visit the sanctuary.

centre where students can learn more about the protection and welfare of domestic and farm animals as well as wildlife.

Mariana's favourite days are when schools send a class of children to the sanctuary to learn about the bears. They always leave with a new interest in wildlife and an enthusiasm to protect Romania's wildlife and environment. One little girl gave a school report on her visit to the bear sanctuary saying that when she grows up she wants to work at the sanctuary just like Mariana.

There is still a lot of work needed on the issues of bear cub rehabilitation and release back to the wild, as it is inevitable that orphaned bear cubs will continue to be found in and around the forests of Romania. These young cubs need specialist care and the sanctuary aims to work with bear specialists to learn more about caring for orphaned bear cubs and how they can be returned to the wild.

The issue of human-bear conflicts, such as the bears coming into towns and villages to eat from rubbish bins, also needs to be dealt with. It is the hope of the Milioane de Prieteni that the Zarnesti bear sanctuary will become a future training centre for students and researchers aiming to protect wildlife through proper scientific studies and practical project work in Romania.

What started in 2005 as a seemingly impossible task, to rescue all the illegally kept captive bears in Romania and to create a positive public awareness and support for the protection of bears in Romania, has turned out far better than Cristina Lapis had dreamed of. The Romanian government has given its legal backing to the rescue of the bears and the Romanian public and the media have shown their support through their continued interest in the daily work at the sanctuary. As for the bears – the sanctuary will ensure they have a long and comfortable life.

FUNDING

The Zarnesti bear sanctuary was designed by the World Society for the Protection of Animals and the initial costs for its construction, the bear rescues, veterinary care, and staff training were provided mainly through the WSPA, who initiated the project with the Romanian organisation the Asociatia Milioane de Prieteni.

All the on-site management of construction work and long-term sanctuary administration has been undertaken by the Asociatia Milioane de Prieteni, whose President is Cristina Lapis. Cristina's organisation manages the bear sanctuary staff who rescue and care for the bears.

The staff also undertake all the necessary maintenance work on the sanctuary enclosures, buildings and surrounding area.

Additional funds for the sanctuary were donated by individuals and various animal protection groups such the German 'Europäischen Tier- und Naturschutz' and the 'Bund Gegen Missbrauch der Tiere' as well as the French organisation 'Bridget Bardot Foundation'.

A number of local Romanian companies donated funds or products, including Carrefour, Real, Metro and Hornbach supermarkets, Dacia, Bricostore, Metabras, Italtruck and Eurocopter Romania.

Anyone wishing to learn more about the bears at the Zarnesti bear sanctuary can visit the web site of the Asociatia Milioane de Prieteni (Millions of Friends) at: **http://www.milioanedeprieteni.org/.**

The sanctuary is known locally as the Libearty Bear Sanctuary, and you can support the rescue of more bears and help care for those already in the sanctuary by making a donation through their web site, or by becoming a 'Friend of the Libearty Bears' at: **http://www.milioanedeprieteni.org/** and receive a paw-marked certificate with photos of the rescued bears.

from left to right: Some of a bear's foods include acorns, hazelnuts and blackberries.
below: In the sanctuary, naturally available foods are supplemented with fruit and vegetables thrown over the perimeter fence.

BEARS' DIET

In the Zarnesti bear sanctuary the rescued bears do still have a wide variety of natural food available to them such as acorns, hazel nuts, blackberries, strawberries, mushrooms, ant nests and all manner of vegetation from leaves to grasses and roots. The bears in the sanctuary are often seen grazing on grass in the meadows and chewing on leaves from surrounding bushes and trees. They can also eat small animals that live in the forest enclosures, such as mice and birds.

But as the forest enclosures are too small to enable all the bears to survive solely off the natural food supply, the sanctuary staff provide a daily supplement of food for the bears in the form of fruit, vegetables and occasionally chicken carcasses. This food is thrown over the perimeter fence at different locations so that the bears have to search for it. This plentiful supply of food means the bears do not have to compete with each other in order to survive and, as a result, there is very little aggression shown towards each other. The sanctuary truly acts like a retirement home for the bears with their food delivered daily and they can snack on the natural food of the forest whenever they feel peckish.

During the late autumn, bears in the wild will feed continually to lay down a heavy layer of body fat which they then use as an energy source to survive during their winter hibernation. In the sanctuary, the bears fatten up on the glut of acorns which rain down from the oak trees in the enclosures. The sanctuary staff supply extra food during this time and, when the snow arrives, most of the bears slowly disappear into the forest to sleep through the winter

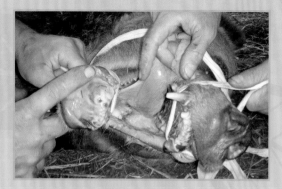

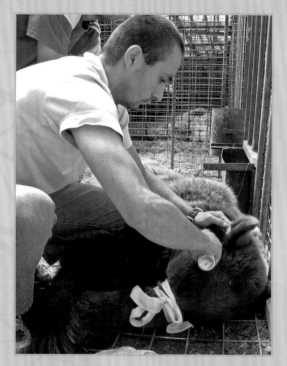

months in their hibernation dens. Usually a few bears stay awake throughout the winter, seeming to enjoy the snow and iced-up pools. The sanctuary staff keep providing food for these bears for as long as they need it.

When the temperature rises and the snow starts to melt, the hibernating bears slowly emerge, a lot lighter in weight than when they started their hibernation. They feed on the new grass and plant shoots and the sanctuary staff ensure there is always a ready supply of extra food available for the foraging bears.

VETERINARY CARE

When a bear is first rescued and brought to the Zarnesti bear sanctuary, it needs to be given a thorough check by the sanctuary vet to see if it has any ailments or injuries which may need immediate attention.

After a period of rest in a warm quarantine den, the bear may be tranquilised to allow the vet to check its eyes, ears, teeth and body for possible injuries or sickness. The bear is weighed and its weight recorded with all the other observations in a veterinary record. At this stage the bear will also have a micro-chip inserted just under the skin near its shoulder. This will enable easy identification of the animal if any future veterinary work needs to be done.

Bears are resilient animals and they are able to survive for years in the direst conditions. In the cages and poor zoos of Romania they survive on meagre diets in cages so small that they can sometimes take only a few paces in any direction before being confronted by the iron bars or concrete barriers to their freedom.

Many of these bears suffer from broken teeth from constantly biting their cage bars. Their paws and claws are often cracked and split due to the damp concrete floors of their cage and their fur may be matted with mud. Their eyesight may be affected due to a diet poor in essential vitamins and minerals, which can cause cataracts and lead to partial or total blindness.

Skin and fur parasites are common as are internal parasites but these can be easily treated with the right medicines. In some cases the animals' teeth can be removed to prevent pain and ongoing abscesses and cracked paws usually heal quickly once the bear is in a more natural environment.

Most bears recover and put on weight quickly in the sanctuary quarantine area. They mainly need time to rest and recuperate in a warm, clean and stress-free environment.

opposite and this page: Bears coming in to the sanctuary are checked by a vet for injuries or sickness and treated.

All the male bears have to be surgically castrated before they can be released into the forested enclosures to mix with other bears. This operation ensures that no breeding will take place in the sanctuary. The male bears are sedated and the vet is able to perform the operation in under an hour. The bear then spends a few days recovering in a quarantine area and after a few weeks is usually ready to mix with the other bears.

Although there is a qualified vet on call for the bears, they very rarely need any further veterinary treatment once they are released into the main forest enclosures.

Brown bears in Romania

EOGRAPHICALLY, ROMANIA IS BOTH A central and south-eastern European country.

The Carpathian Mountain Range, which spreads through Romania and neighbouring countries, is a well preserved forested region of mountains and hills which the brown bear, as well as the wolf and European lynx, has inhabited for thousands of years.

There are estimated to be around 6,000 brown bears in Romania today, representing 35% of the total number found in the whole of Europe outside the Russian territory, and is the largest European population of this species.

Little is known about the historical situation of the bear in Romania. During World War II they were heavily hunted and after the war less than 1,000 bears were believed to be left in the wild.

In the 1960s, the management of this species changed dramatically. The dictator Nicolae Ceausescu was a passionate bear hunter and he ensured that only he and his friends had the right to hunt them. During his regime, bears were strictly protected and anyone else who killed a bear without his agreement could end up in prison with a fine equivalent of two years' salary at that time.

Bears were provided with extra food in Ceausescu's favourite hunting areas to encourage their breeding and to ensure there were always bears in the area to hunt. To get the best trophies, Ceausescu would hang pieces of meat from trees so that only bears taller than 2 metres could reach it and as these huge male bears were the main target of his hunting sprees, it was not long before large bears became rare in that area.

In 1974 Ceausescu had 30 bear cubs caught from the wild and kept in an enclosure for a year where they were well fed on meat and vegetables, after which the bears were released into the hunting grounds. Over 500 bears were 'farmed' in this way to supply Ceausescu's hunting friends with easy prey. Due to the restrictions on hunting and the release into the wild of captive raised bears the Romanian bear population grew extremely fast, reaching a peak of over 7,000 animals by 1988.

In March 1990, three months after the fall of Ceausescu, the Romanian government re-opened the bear hunt to the public. When the number of bears in the wild started to fall, the government decided to impose hunting quotas to ensure a healthy wild bear population remained, as foreign hunters were eager to pay high prices to hunt bear in Romania.

Brown bear habitat in Romania covers an area of about 69,000 sq km, mostly in the Carpathian Mountains. The distribution of brown bears in Romania has remained constant over the last two decades, with around 6,000 bears in the wild. Around 300 bears are hunted legally each year, some by foreign hunters paying for the 'sport', but many bears are also killed illegally by poachers.

The nature of brown bears

BROWN BEARS (*URSUS ARCTOS*) ARE THE most widespread of the 8 living bear species. They are found across North America, Europe, northern Russia and Asia as far as Japan.

There are around 200,000 brown bears left in the wild but they are threatened by habitat destruction and in many countries they are hunted for trophies or killed as pests when they destroy farmers' crops or beehives or when they come into towns to feed from rubbish bins.

Brown bears living in European countries are known as European brown bears, and they are generally smaller in size than the American brown bears (also known as Grizzlies), but they are all the same species, known as *Ursus arctos*.

EUROPEAN BROWN BEAR
(*Ursus arctos*)

LIFESPAN: 20 to 25 years in the wild.

SIZE: Adult males can measure up to 2 metres in length.

WEIGHT: Adult males can weigh from 135 kg to over 250 kg.
Adult females weigh 95 kg to 200 kg.

APPEARANCE
The fur of European brown bears varies from light to dark brown in colour. They have a distinctive hump of muscle over the shoulder which gives great power to their front limbs for digging when they are searching for food or digging a hibernation den. Long claws on the front paws are effective tools for digging and also for climbing trees.

HABITAT & DISTRIBUTION

The brown bear is the most widespread of the world's eight bear species, ranging across North America, Europe, Northern Russia and Asia and into the northern island of Hokkaido in Japan.

Today, bears are rare in Western Europe. They have been hunted in large numbers and their forest habitat destroyed due to the expansion of agriculture, towns and cities. This has left only small populations in countries such as Greece, Spain, Italy and France, with larger populations in Scandinavia and some Balkan countries.

In Romania around 6,000 brown bears live in the deciduous forests on the slopes of the Carpathian Mountains. The bears may also come down into the valleys in search of food.

REPRODUCTION

Male and female brown bears reach sexual maturity at 4 to 7 years of age. Mating takes place from early May to mid-July but implantation of the fertilized egg into the uterus does not occur until October or November – this is known as 'delayed implantation'. This delay in the fertilized egg developing into an embryo and then into a baby bear is a miracle of evolution as it means the baby bear does not begin its development inside its mother's uterus until the mother is safely tucked up in her hibernation den. Between one and four cubs are born between January and March, while the mother bear is still in her hibernation den. The cubs remain with their mothers for two years before venturing off to claim their own territory.

DIET

Brown bears are omnivorous (eat both plants and animals) but around 85% of their diet is made up of plants. They feed on grass, herbs, roots, bulbs and flowers, and switch to berries and fruits when they ripen, and acorns, beechnuts, chestnuts and hazelnuts in the autumn. Brown bears also eat insects, fungi, fish, honey and small mammals, and will eat animal carcasses when they come across them. In some areas they also prey on livestock such as sheep. Brown bears congregate at high densities where food is abundant, such as at salmon streams, but also at garbage dumps near their forest habitat where they feed on the scraps of food people throw away.

HIBERNATION

Natural plant foods can be difficult to find during the long cold winter periods, but brown bears have evolved an amazing survival strategy – they sleep for 3 to 4 months until the snows have gone and food is easy to find again. This winter sleep is called hibernation and involves the bear fattening up on a high calorie diet before winter and then living off this fat store while sleeping for several months in a warm den of earth or under old trees and occasionally in caves. During hibernation, bears reduce their body temperature and their breathing rate and heart rate drops. They do not normally eat, urinate or defecate during their long hibernation. Mothers give birth to their cubs while in the hibernation den and the cubs emerge with their mother when the weather improves, around March or April.

The 'trash bin' bears

ROUND 6,000 BEARS LIVE IN THE WILD IN the forests and mountains of Romania where they find a wide variety of natural food. But their forest habitat is becoming increasingly encroached upon by the expanding towns, cities and agricultural land.

This can restrict the bears' natural territory and natural food resources but can offer easier and different food sources as the bears are tempted out of the forest to search in rubbish bins, on farms, in orchards and campsites.

Bears searching for food can cause damage to property or to farm produce. If they come too close to where people are living, they may also be seen as potentially dangerous animals and classified as 'nuisance' bears. That can result in the bears being killed.

If mother bears with cubs are targeted as 'nuisance' bears, the cubs may be left orphaned in the wild and die of starvation or may be captured and placed into zoos or into private ownership where they may suffer a life of poor welfare and distress.

Bears are highly intelligent opportunistic feeders and they know an easy meal when they see (or smell) one. When their forest home is right next to a farmer's fruit orchard or maize field or even next to rubbish bins laden with discarded human food, they see no reason not to make good use of this new food source, as long as they can overcome their fear of people. This can cause what is termed as a human-bear conflict situation.

The city of Brasov is surrounded by the forested Carpathian Mountains. 300,000 people live in the city but around 300 brown bears live in the forests surrounding Brasov and neighbouring towns, so it is not surprising to learn that some of these bears search for food in and around the outskirts of the city.

There is an area of Brasov called Racadau where many apartment blocks have been built very close to the edge of the surrounding forest. For the past 10 or more years, bears have regularly come out of the forest at night to feed in the large open metal trash bins that serve the apartment blocks.

The problem is that some people like to watch the bears and even entice them to come closer. They take photos and tell their friends about the bears and before long the sight of a bear sitting in a trash bin on the edge of the town has become a tourist attraction. The lack of negative action towards the bears encourages the animals to see little threat from people and that is what can eventually lead to a real conflict situation, where man and bear can become injured, or even killed.

The wild bears visiting trash bins at Racadau had become a popular tourist attraction, with cars and taxis taking tourists to see the sight. In 2005 the situation got out of hand when people

opposite page: A bear searches for food amongst the rubbish people have left.

started trying to hand-feed these wild animals and someone was injured by a mother bear protecting her cubs near the bins. The Mayor of Brasov decided it was time to take action, which meant possibly having to kill the bears.

Around the same time a female bear had been found dead next to the bins and an autopsy showed she had 18 plastic bags in her stomach as a result of eating them with the food they contained from the nearby bins.

Something had to be done to prevent the bears from eating human garbage, not only to protect the people, but also to protect the bears.

Luckily for the bears, efforts were made by local animal groups to find other ways of keeping the bears away from the bins, rather than killing them. The WSPA, who were helping to create the bear sanctuary at Zarnesti, offered to help resolve the human-bear conflict situation at Racadau by designing some bear-proof rubbish bins. These allowed the public to open the

bin and deposit their rubbish bags but the bears were unable to open the bins.

The rubbish disposal company which was servicing Brasov at that time also contributed to the project and they brought in a number of large bear-proof containers to the area. In addition, local wildlife groups started a public awareness campaign aimed at informing the residents at Racadau how they should use the new bins while also alerting them to the potential fines for incorrect rubbish disposal. A team of local students spent the next 6 months monitoring the rubbish sites at night to ensure that tourists were kept away from the area. If taxis came along with tourists, the students would call the police, who promptly drove in and warned the taxis to keep away.

Another part of the project was to trap the bears which were coming down to the bin areas and to re-locate them hundreds of kilometres away. This was undertaken by local biologists

Something had to be done …
not only to protect the people,
but also to protect the bears.

who also radio-collared the bears to monitor their movements after release.

At the beginning of the project in 2006 there were around 40 bears regularly coming to the Racadau area to feed in the bins. By 2009 there were only 4 or 5 bears coming occasionally to check the bin areas, so the problem had been greatly reduced.

But this sort of project needs to be continued for the long term as bears will start returning if rubbish is left exposed. Elsewhere in Romania there are a number of areas where bears are attracted to human food sources, especially around hotels and restaurants located in or near forests. In some cases the hotels and restaurants are directly responsible for attracting the bears to their doorstep by leaving out food to ensure

above: Posters are put up to make people aware of bears frequenting the area.

the bears come close so the hotel guests can take photos. The authorities are now trying to clamp down on these foolish activities.

Bear cub rehabilitation

THE ZARNESTI BEAR SANCTUARY WAS SET up to care for bears which had been caught from the wild as cubs and had spent many years in captivity. There were some sub-adult bears, of 2 to 3 years of age, but most rescued bears were adult and elderly animals.

There was no other option but to keep them in the forested sanctuary enclosures for the rest of their lives, with the sanctuary acting much like a retirement home for the rescued bears.

So why can't these bears be released back to the wild in the Carpathian Mountains?

The simple answer is that these rescued bears would be unlikely to survive in the wild as many have health problems such as broken teeth from the constant biting on the bars of their cages. Also, the bears have relied on their human owners feeding them in captivity and so have become too accustomed to people. There would be the risk that, if released into the wild, they would have little fear of people and would seek out easier food sources around human habitations, becoming nuisance bears which would usually result in them being killed.

As the public got to learn about the bear sanctuary, bear cubs – some as young as a few months old – were brought to Zarnesti in the hope that the sanctuary would care for them. It is illegal to catch bear cubs from the wild in Romania but a few cubs were 'found' every year, probably as a result of hunters killing the mother bear, but also due to other reasons. Mothers sometimes become parted from their offspring near busy roads or when seeking out food in and around the towns bordering their forests. Also, mothers have been known to abandon the cubs if natural food supplies are scarce.

Very young bear cubs have a 'teddy-bear' cuteness and appeal which is usually what attracts people to 'rescuing' them and keeping them as a pet. But this lasts only for a short time and by 7 months of age a bear cub is already outgrowing the size and strength of a domestic dog. People who obtain a bear cub as a pet soon realise their mistake when it rapidly increases in size and strength to become a dangerous animal to have in the house.

Orphaned bear cubs are found all over the world where bears live in proximity to human

below: An orphaned bear cub is taken into care at an Idaho sanctuary.

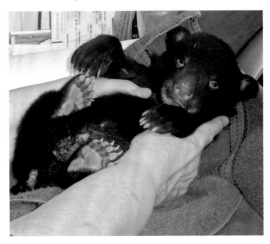

habitation. In the past, if an orphaned cub was found it would usually be kept as a caged pet or it may have ended up in a zoo or a circus. But there is now another option, which is to care for the cub until it is old enough to be returned back to the wild, a process known as rehabilitation.

Contrary to popular belief, bear cubs do not need to learn survival skills from their mother. They are perfectly capable of learning to live in the wild by using their natural wild instincts. They test plants, insects, meat etc. to see if they are edible and they instinctively know how to climb trees and dig hibernation dens, how to dig for roots and insects and how to search for wild bees-nests full of honey.

However, they do need protection in the wild until they are old enough and strong enough to look after themselves and are able to escape predators, including adult male bears. Their mother is that protection and the cubs normally stay with their mother for around 2 years before setting off on their own. If they lose their mother before reaching at least 8 months of age they may not survive in the wild.

There are now a number of projects set up around the world to rehabilitate orphaned bear cubs and release them back to the wild. But caring for young bear cubs is a specialised job and has to be done correctly. Minimal contact with humans is needed during the rehabilitation process.

Very young cubs need to be bottle fed with a milk substitute several times a day for the first few months of their lives. By 5 or 6 months of age, they will start to eat solid food such as fruits, vegetables, nuts, leaves and later on a little meat.

Some orphaned cubs, when found, may be suffering from malnutrition, injuries or may have infections. Veterinary treatment and vaccinations can usually bring them back to good health.

Cubs need to be kept in safe enclosures such as in small areas of natural forest surrounded by fences which prevent them from climbing out. Here they can practice climbing and digging. It is also important to allow cubs to socialize with other orphaned cubs as they learn from each other through play.

Young bears can be released back to the wild from around 1 year of age, by which time they have put on sufficient body weight and muscle. It is important to ensure that the forest where they are released has adequate natural food resources and is far away from towns and villages.

Prior to release, the young bears may have to be tranquilised and a radio collar fitted around their neck, a microchip inserted under their skin and an ear tag attached to their ear. These are used by researchers to monitor the bears after release.

By using radio-telemetry, the researcher can pick up signals from the radio collar and learn where the bear is travelling. This can also be used to show if the bear is coming near to human habitation, in which case the bear may need to be recaptured and moved further away.

The Zarnesti bear sanctuary did not have the facilities to rehabilitate the first few young bear cubs which were brought into the sanctuary, so those cubs will have to remain in the forest enclosures. However, in future, any cubs brought in will be sent to a new project in the north of Romania where they can be properly rehabilitated and released back to the wild in the depths of the mountain forests.

Bears in captivity

A LL SPECIES OF BEARS CAN BE FOUND IN poor captive conditions around the world. Over fifteen thousand bears are kept in cages for their entire lives in Asian Bear Farms where the farmers regularly extract bile from the living bears' gall bladders to make medicines, tonics and cosmetic products. In India and Pakistan hundreds of bears have been caught from the wild to be cruelly trained as dancing bears, to gain money from tourists wanting a snapshot of the bears on the streets. In Pakistan, bears are even tied to ropes in arenas to fight powerful dogs in illegal bear-baiting events.

Countless thousands of bears are kept in zoos around the world, in cages and enclosures which are often totally inappropriate for providing the animals with sufficient enrichment for them to exhibit their natural behaviour. Circuses keep bears captive in small cages and transport them from town to town and country to country in so-called Beast-Wagons, which are basically small cages on a lorry. Apart from their poor captive environment, these animals are often trained by cruel methods to perform unnatural actions, such as riding bicycles, balancing on balls etc. for the entertainment of paying visitors.

In many countries bear cubs are caught from the wild, or found orphaned, and then kept as pets. As the cubs quickly grow out of their cute stage, they are then often neglected and live a miserable life in featureless cages.

Bears are intelligent animals and in the wild live highly complex lives. In their natural environment, individual bears generally have tens, sometimes hundreds, of square kilometres of territory which they cover in search of food and mates.

Placing them in restrictive captive conditions can seriously affect their mental and physical wellbeing. Stereotypic behaviour (where the animals make repetitive movements such as pacing and rocking) is commonly seen in such captive animals and is a clear indication of physical and mental stress.

There are serious concerns about the welfare of the thousands of bears in captivity across the world. To improve the welfare of these animals there are several options available, assuming the bears could be released from their current poor state.

RELEASE TO THE WILD

The ideal solution for these animals would be to release them back into their wild natural habitat, where they would be free to exhibit all their natural behaviours. However, this is not an option in the majority of cases due to the age, psychological and physical condition of the animals and the lack of suitable release sites.

BEAR SANCTUARIES

If the bears cannot be released back to the wild, the next best option is to let the bears live in large forested areas such as bear sanctuaries which are enclosed by physical barriers to prevent them escaping into the wild. This provides the animals with large natural areas and sufficient enrichment for them to exhibit their natural behaviours.

ZOOS

Failing the availability of large forested sanctuaries, bears in extremely poor captive conditions could be moved to zoos. Although the living conditions for animals in many zoos around the world are less than adequate, there are exceptions, and for an animal previously confined to a small cage with a poor diet and no veterinary care, placing the bear into the care of a good zoo could be beneficial for the animal's welfare.

Bear sanctuaries around the world

A KEY ELEMENT OF THE WORK TO PROTECT bears from cruelty in captivity over the past two decades has been the creation of naturally forested 'sanctuary' enclosures.

Bear sanctuaries make it possible for the authorities to eradicate illegal or cruel use of bears, such as dancing bears, bear-baiting and the illegal trade in bears, as they offer a safe and suitable home for the rescued animals. The sanctuary provides an environment similar to the bears' natural habitat and allows them to display their natural behaviour such as climbing, swimming, digging and hibernating.

The World Society for the Protection of Animals (WSPA) created the first bear sanctuary in Greece in 1992 and has since helped to build others in Turkey, Hungary, Thailand, Laos, Pakistan, India and Romania. All of these

sanctuaries were donated to local organisations or municipalities to manage after completion of the initial construction and bear rescue work, but the WSPA remained available to advise on technical aspects of sanctuary management as required.

This concept has been so successful that over the past decade a number of other organisations have developed sanctuaries for rescued bears in countries such as China, Vietnam, Cambodia, Bulgaria and Germany. The following pages describe some of these bear sanctuaries but there are new sanctuaries being developed each year, so the issue of bears being kept in poor captive conditions is one that is realistically being addressed. The sanctuaries are raising public awareness of the need to protect bears and their natural habitat for the future.

GREECE
DANCING BEARS

The first major project supported by WSPA's 'Libearty Campaign' in 1992 was the eradication of the cruel practice of dancing bears in Greece. Only a couple of hundred European brown bears live in the forests of northern Greece, and hunters had been illegally killing mother bears to get the cubs. The cubs were sold to local gypsies who had a centuries-old tradition of training these bears to 'dance'.

The young bears were trained to 'dance' by making them stand on hot metal sheets, to force them to get up on their hind paws and shuffle around as if dancing. Meanwhile the gypsy owner would play music on a tambourine or violin so the bear would learn to stand up when it heard the music, associating it with the pain in its paws.

The bears were restrained by chains punched through their sensitive noses and were taken onto the streets by their gypsy owners, trying to get tourists to pay for a holiday snapshot of the bears. The bears would stand up and shuffle around when the owner tugged at the chain, sending painful shocks through the animal's nose. If the bears refused to stand they would be beaten on their legs with clubs.

The Greek government had been receiving hundreds of complaints from tourists concerned about the cruelty to bears on the streets of Athens. In 1992 the Greek Ministry of Environment accepted the advice and help offered by WSPA in an effort to find a solution to the problem of the dancing bear trade.

Apart from the illegality of capturing the bears from the wild (they are a protected species in Greece), laws had been in place since 1969 prohibiting the killing, possession or public exhibition of bears. But until the WSPA intervention, the Greek authorities had felt powerless to stop the use of the dancing bears.

The problem had always been a lack of facilities to accommodate the animals following confiscation, making enforcement of the law impossible. The bear sanctuary changed all that.

THE SANCTUARY

The WSPA developed the concept of the world's first bear sanctuary as an innovative method for providing a natural environment for rescued bears in Greece. They designed and helped finance and build a veterinary care centre and a

above: Not always a happy ending. Dimitri was in serious pain, was blind and his body was racked with infection when he was rescued. It was decided the kindest thing to do was to euthanize the old bear.

forest bear sanctuary in northern Greece, working with a newly created Greek wildlife organisation called Arcturos.

During 1992 WSPA and Arcturos investigated the locations of dancing bears. When not being used on the streets of the main towns and cities, the bears were kept in appalling conditions in gypsy camps. They were constantly chained up or caged and it was clear they were poorly fed.

A 3 hectare area of beech forest high up in mountains of northern Greece was used to create the first bear sanctuary, a few kilometres from a small village called Nympheo. This was prime brown bear habitat, a perfect place for rescued bears to regain their natural behaviours after years of captivity.

The sanctuary enclosure and veterinary clinic were part-funded by a Greek winemaker – Yiannis Boutaris, who had joined forces with

Dimitri's owners had chained him up
in a deserted building to slowly die.

the WSPA in their efforts to eradicate the dancing bear trade from Greece. Boutari helped create the Arcturos organisation which was to manage the bear sanctuary after completion.

In January 1993 the first dancing bears were rescued. A team of specialists from WSPA and Arcturos were supported by Greek police and staff from the Ministry of the Environment in confiscating bears from gypsy camps on the outskirts of Athens and Thessaloniki.

The first bear to be rescued was a 5 year old female brown bear called Mary. She was kept in a cage so small she had to crawl into it. The gypsy camp where this bear was kept was considered so dangerous a place that the Greek police gave the rescue team an armed escort into the camp at dawn. The team had to work fast to get the bear out of its tiny cage and into a transport crate as the growing crowd of gypsies became increasingly aggressive and even the police did not want to stay there longer than necessary.

Mary had a colourful noseband tied tightly around her muzzle in the fashion of many dancing bears. When this was removed at the sanctuary clinic she was found to have several massive abscesses which had erupted through her jaw and nose. The leather muzzle was clearly meant to hide this severe and painful injury from view.

The bear was freed from her chains and given veterinary care. Within weeks she had changed from a small and fragile animal to a healthy bear.

The next bear rescued was a 27 year old male bear called Dimitri. He was old and blind and so diseased he could hardly stand. His owners had chained him up in a deserted building to slowly die. When he was brought back to the sanctuary clinic the vet tranquilised him and, after an inspection, it was clear the bear was in serious pain. His eye sockets were weeping with infection, his teeth were falling out of his gums and his body was a bag of bones. The vet made the sad decision to euthanize the old bear to put him out of his misery.

The WSPA provided financial and technical support to the Greek bear sanctuary for the next 3 years before Arcturos took over full management of the facility. Dancing bears were eradicated from Greece within 2 years of the sanctuary becoming operational, so the project was a complete success.

The Arcturos bear sanctuary now cares for 15 bears, including an American black bear rescued from a circus and 3 bears from the Belgrade zoo, brought in after the Yugoslavian wars.

Arcturos has developed a visitor and wildlife awareness centre in the nearby town of Amindeo and over 50,000 people visit the bear sanctuary each year. In addition, Arcturos undertakes nationwide wildlife awareness programmes through schools and funds a variety of scientific studies on bears in the wild in Greece and neighbouring countries.

TURKEY
DANCING BEARS

Dancing bears had been a common sight in tourist areas of Turkey for many years but in 1992 the Turkish government agreed to work with the WSPA to eradicate the cruel exploitation of bears. The government was concerned that the increasing number of complaints from tourists about the bears was affecting their emerging tourist industry. They were also aware that the WSPA was working productively with the Greek government to eradicate dancing bears in Greece.

Throughout 1992 and 1993 investigations into the use of dancing bears in Turkey showed there were around 50 brown bears being used mainly in tourist hot-spots in Istanbul and in several Turkish beach resorts.

These bears had been taken from the wild as cubs, which meant the mother bears would have been killed to get them. Although there are around 3,000 European brown bears in the wild in Turkey, they are a protected species. It is illegal to catch them from the wild and to use

them in public places. The Turkish authorities had been unable to enforce this law as they had nowhere to keep any confiscated bears.

The young bears were trained to 'dance' by cruel methods similar to those used by gypsies in Greece. The cubs had chains piercing their noses and other chains around their necks to restrain them. One tug on the nose-chain was enough to make the powerful animals wince with pain and submit to their human trainers.

There were several areas in Istanbul where the dancing bears were used to attract custom from tourists. The main area was outside one of the biggest tourist attractions, the Dolmabache Palace, which was once the residence of the Ottoman Sultans.

The WSPA investigators found that the gypsies actually lived in a camp outside the city, but their bears were kept chained up in a park

previous page: Rescued bears at the Turkish bear sanctuary.

near to the Palace. Each day the gypsies came into the city, unchained their bears from the trees in the park, and took them to the streets around the Palace where the tourist buses would arrive. After several hours the gypsies would have earned sufficient money from tourists paying for snapshots of the bears and the animals would be taken back into the park and chained up once more.

The park was a public area with families walking through it all day but hidden out of sight in a wooded area, there were over a dozen adult brown bears. They spent over 20 hours each day chained to trees there, with nothing to eat apart from stale bread crusts.

Other bears were regularly chained up on rocks just outside the city and each day they would be unchained and taken to other tourist areas, such as the famous Topkapi Palace, where tourists would pay $10 or more to take a photo of them. These bears spent up to 20 hours a day tethered by short chains to the rocks in all weathers, with only dry bread for food.

In 1993 the WSPA built a bear veterinary care centre at Uludag University near Bursa, a few hundred kilometres from Istanbul, and later built a 5 hectare bear sanctuary enclosure in pine forests nearby, on land provided by the Turkish Ministry of Forestry. The sanctuary had large water pools and hibernation dens and the forest area was surrounded by tall weld-mesh fences protected by electric wires. In October 1993 a dozen dancing bears

were confiscated from the streets of Istanbul and taken to the bear care centre to undergo a period of rehabilitation and veterinary treatment before being released into the large forest sanctuary enclosure. More bears were confiscated by the Turkish authorities in the following months and by 1995 there were no more dancing bears in Turkey. The Turkish bear sanctuary had 50 rescued bears in its care and all were doing well.

The WSPA and a local Turkish animal group, called the Turkiye Hayvanlari Koruma Dernegi (THKD), supported the Turkish government in running the sanctuary until 2000 when the management was handed over to a team from the nearby Uludag University. The sanctuary is still under the control of the Turkish Ministry of Forestry.

A second forest enclosure was added to the sanctuary in 2007 to double the size of the forest area available to the 50 bears now living there. Some of the older dancing bears have died over the past decade and a half since their rescue from the streets of Istanbul but a number of orphaned bear cubs found in the Turkish forests have been taken to the sanctuary in recent years.

The Turkish bear sanctuary enabled the authorities to enforce the law and confiscate all dancing bears in the country. There have been no dancing bears seen on the streets of Turkey since 1995, so the project was a complete success in stopping this cruel trade.

above: A sun bear.

THAILAND
ILLEGAL TRADE IN BEARS

There are two bear species living in the wild in Thailand and neighbouring countries, the Asiatic black bear and the sun bear. These two species of bear had been caught and illegally traded in Thailand, sometimes for the exotic pet trade but also for their gall bladders, their paws and even for their meat, which had been sold illegally in restaurants. During the 1990s the Thai wildlife authorities (Thai Royal Forestry Department – RFD) had worked hard to combat this trade and it had necessitated the confiscation of many animals.

A change in Thai law in the early 1990s made the keeping of wild animals as pets illegal, which resulted in many species of wildlife being handed in to the RFD's wildlife rescue centres or dumped at Buddhist Temples around the country.

In 1995 the RFD had confiscated 20 Asiatic bears from illegal trade and built small cages for

above: Rescued bears enjoying a refreshing dip at one of the Thai bear sanctuaries.

them at their Wildlife Rescue Centre at Bangla-mung, south of Bangkok. This put a strain on their resources and would have prevented them confiscating further animals if the WSPA had not stepped in to help.

The WSPA agreed to design and fund the building of a bear sanctuary to provide better living conditions for the rescued bears and also to enable the RFD to continue to confiscate bears from illegal trade.

The first 5 hectare sanctuary enclosure was built in 1996 at Banglamung in south east Thailand. The RFD moved the rescued Asiatic black bears from the cages into the forested enclosure and then were able to undertake more confiscations of bears in need of rescue. A second sanctuary enclosure was then built to care for rescued sun bears, which were also found in illegal trade. The enclosures had water pools and shaded den areas in amongst the natural forest vegetation and the bears were fed daily with a mixture of rice and vegetables.

Several other smaller bear sanctuaries were built in northern Thailand around 1998 to accommodate Asiatic bears confiscated from illegal trade in that region of the country.

The Thai bear sanctuaries are all owned and managed by the Thai Royal Forestry Department (RFD) and have been supported by the Thai Society for the Conservation of Wild Animals (TSCWA), who organised the building of the bear sanctuaries with funding from the WSPA, and who have provided on-site veterinary advice and maintenance, working alongside the RFD.

The sanctuaries are on Government land and are not open to the general public but they occasionally allow school groups access for educational purposes and to create awareness of the need for bear protection in rural areas.

The WSPA agreed to design and fund the building of a bear sanctuary to provide better living conditions for the rescued bears.

HUNGARY
CAPTIVE BEARS

The WSPA designed and funded the construction of a bear sanctuary in Hungary in 1998 after hearing of 21 brown bears being kept in appalling captive conditions. The bears had been used by the Hungarian film industry for over a decade and had been kept in small cages on a plot of land near the town of Godollo, 50 km north of Budapest.

There are no bears in the wild in Hungary and most of these captive bears had been brought into the country illegally while some had been obtained from local zoos and circuses. Despite the efforts of their former animal trainer to look after them, the conditions in which these animals were being kept were poor, with animals living in small cages with limited food.

The Mayor of Veresegyhaz, a town near to Godollo, agreed to provide the land for the bear sanctuary on the outskirts of the town and also to take on the management of the sanctuary. A 3 hectare enclosure was built with a number of dens in which the bears could hibernate, as well as two large fresh water pools in which they could swim. An office, storerooms, a food preparation area and quarantine dens are also located on the site.

below: Having a snooze in the cool shade.

above and below: Two of the rescued bears at home in the Hungarian sanctuary.

Following the opening of the sanctuary in 1998, more bears were rescued from captivity in Hungary and one rescued bear was even brought from the Ukraine. In 2005 the WSPA negotiated with the Mayor of Limassol in Cyprus to free two brown bears from their life of captivity in a damp concrete enclosure at Limassol Zoo. These two bears were brought to the Hungarian bear sanctuary and a new quarantine area was built to accommodate them. The new quarantine area will also be used to care for sick or injured bears and to take in new bears as the need arises. By 2010 there were 40 brown bears in the sanctuary.

The sanctuary is open to the public who can walk around the perimeter fence to observe the bears in the woodland enclosure. In 2010 an education centre was created next to the sanctuary where visitors and local school children can learn about wildlife and animal protection. The 3 hectare sanctuary will also be doubled in size as soon as funds become available to develop the forest area behind the first enclosure.

above: An Indian dancing bear.

INDIA
DANCING BEARS

In 1995 the WSPA initiated the first ever investigation into the trade in dancing bears in India. The investigation, funded by WSPA and undertaken by a wildlife organisation based in Delhi called Wildlife SOS, revealed there were more than 1,000 sloth bears used as dancing bears on the streets of India and that over 100 sloth bear cubs were being caught from the wild annually to fuel this trade.

The sloth bear cubs had their teeth pulled out, a hole pierced through their muzzle and a rope threaded through the hole, by which the bear would be tethered and controlled for the rest of its life. The animal is forced to stand up and dance by its Kalandar (Gypsy) owner pulling on the rope, causing severe pain to the animal. Although bears had been used in this way in towns and villages of India for centuries, by the 1990s the practice had spread to major tourist sites, such as around the Taj Mahal, near Agra in northern India.

The Indian government agreed that this was an illegal practice but said confiscation of bears was not an option unless there was a purpose-built facility to care for them.

The WSPA provided funds and design for the creation of a bear sanctuary within the Sur Sarovar wildlife centre near Agra and it was ready to take in confiscated bears by 2002. The aim was to enable the Indian government and the Wildlife SOS group to confiscate dancing bears being used along the tourist route leading to Agra (where the Taj Mahal is located) and to work with Kalandar communities to provide them with alternative livelihoods and so phase out the use of dancing bears in the area.

Further sanctuaries and a wider, holistic project would be needed to completely eradicate the trade in dancing bears in India, but the Indian government showed great interest in the project and appeared supportive of developing further sanctuaries.

The Agra sanctuary forest enclosure was initially 6 hectares in size and totally surrounded by a 2.8 metres high stone wall, fitted with an internal electric fence. As the species of bear held in the sanctuary (sloth bears) are exceptionally good diggers, the foundations of the wall extended over 1.5 metres into the ground. The sanctuary had quarantine dens, a clinic room and staff quarters as well as a large forested enclosure containing a number of large pools and shelters for the rescued bears.

When the sanctuary was ready to take in bears in 2002, the WSPA donated the sanctuary to the Wildlife SOS group who were working in collaboration with the Uttar Pradesh Forest Department. At the same time, the WSPA encouraged other international wildlife organi-

By 2010 there were believed to be
less than 50 dancing bears still
being used on the streets of India.

sations to provide funding for the ongoing care
of bears in the sanctuary. In recent years the
Agra bear sanctuary has been well supported by
organisations such as the International Animal
Rescue, Free the Bears Fund, One Voice and the
Humane Society International.

The Wildlife SOS has since increased the
size of its sanctuary and has rescued hundreds
of bears. They have helped create additional

bear sanctuaries in India, such as in Bhopal and
at Bannerghatta in the south of the country and
other Indian organisations, such as the Wildlife
Trust of India, have also concentrated on helping to eradicate this trade.

below: A dancing bear chained and waiting
for its next performance.

above: A bear-baiting arena in Pakistan.

The Kalander gypsies have traditionally trained dancing bears for over 400 years and, taking away their bears would take away the livelihood from many of these rural communities, which is why the organisations working to eradicate the use of dancing bears are concentrating on providing alternative livelihoods for the Kalanders. This is working well. By 2010 there were believed to be less than 50 dancing bears still being used on the streets of India and their rescue will bring the history of dancing bears in India to an end.

PAKISTAN
BEAR-BAITING

Bear-baiting was a common form of entertainment in mediaeval Europe and many inns around England would have held bear-baiting as well as bull baiting events in their yards. The cruel sport was made illegal in Britain in 1835.

Pakistan is the only country where bear-baiting still takes place today. Asiatic black bears are caught from the wild and sold to gypsy communities known as Kalandars, who train them as dancing bears. Some dancing bears are also trained to fight dogs and are used for bear-baiting events in certain areas of the country.

In bear-baiting, the bear is tethered by a length of rope to a stake in the ground and two fighting dogs are set on it. The bear tries to fight off the dogs while the dogs try to pull the bear down by going for its muzzle. Each event takes several minutes but during that time both the bear and dogs receive serious injuries. The events are watched by crowds of spectators.

When the WSPA uncovered hundreds of bear-baiting events taking place throughout Pakistan in the mid 1990s, they presented a report documenting the issue to the Pakistan

In bear-baiting, the bear is tethered by a length of rope to a stake in the ground and two fighting dogs are set on it.

government with a call to ban the cruel and illegal events. Bear-baiting is illegal under Pakistan's animal welfare and wildlife laws and is also illegal under Islamic law, which forbids people from making animals fight. Yet the events were difficult to eradicate because they were organised by high-ranking Landlords, who were wealthy and influential governors of their regions and they believed they were above the law.

In 2000 the WSPA built a bear sanctuary with a 5 hectare forest enclosure in the North West Frontier Province (NWFP) of Pakistan, in an area called Kund Park. It was built on request of the NWFP wildlife authorities who would not have been able to confiscate baiting bears without having the sanctuary to accommodate them. Now the bears could be legally confiscated with the help of a local wildlife organisation called the Bio-resource Research Centre, who investigate and uncover the illegal events and also oversee the care of the bears at the sanctuary.

The rescued bears underwent veterinary treatment at the sanctuary as most had serious injuries to their muzzles. After a period of quarantine they were released into the 5 hectare forested sanctuary to enjoy the freedom of trees, earth and water pools. The sanctuary was managed by the NWFP authorities.

Sadly, in July 2010, the Kund Park bear sanctuary was destroyed by the massive flash floods that swept over the north west of Pakistan,

killing thousands of people and livestock and washing away whole villages, leaving millions homeless. Twenty bears were drowned despite heroic efforts on the part of Fakhar Abbas and his team of sanctuary staff to protect the bears and the sanctuary from the floods.

Three bears were miraculously rescued and moved to a new bear sanctuary which was built near to Islamabad, far from the areas affected by flooding. This sanctuary will be used to house all the remaining baiting and dancing bears in Pakistan once they are legally confiscated. The Kalandars are being encouraged to give up using bears by offering them alternative livelihoods with government support.

opposite page: The illegal and ugly face of bear-baiting. Bears and dogs sustain horrific and often fatal injuries.
below: After having their injuries treated and spending some time in quarantine, the rescued bears are released into the sanctuary.

above: A bear farm in China – the bears suffer a lifetime of extreme confinement causing physical and mental distress.

CHINA

BEAR FARMING

The Animals Asia Foundation (AAF) built a bear sanctuary in the Sichuan Province of China in 2001 to care for Asiatic black bears from bear farms which had closed down. These bears had been kept in terrible captive conditions, mainly in small cages, for the purpose of draining bile from their gall bladders to produce medicines and products such as shampoos, toothpastes, tonics and wines.

Around 200 Asiatic black bears were being cared for at the AAF sanctuary in China by late 2010. All these bears needed surgery and intensive care to bring them back to good health. In the farms, the bile is drained daily through tubes leading from the bear's gall bladder. Many of the rescued bears have been found to suffer severe infections due to their poor treatment in the farms.

Bear farming is a legal industry in China and is supported by the Chinese government. Although the Chinese government has actively closed down small unregistered farms and sent over 200 bears to the AAF sanctuary, the government continues to support the expansion and development of the bear farm industry. Despite the closure of many farms, the number of bears held in registered Chinese bear farms today is rising and may be well over 12,000. Bears are bred on the farms but there is also an illegal trade in bear cubs captured from the wild in China and neighbouring countries and sold to the farms.

The sale of bear bile is a commercial success in China, despite there being many traditional herbal medicines which can easily be used in its place. Animal welfare is, unfortunately, still not the priority it should be in the country but organisations such as the AAF and WSPA are

above: A bear farm in Vietnam – this shows the cramped conditions the bears are forced to live in.

campaigning for an end to the farming of bears because of the suffering the animals endure.

The AAF bear sanctuary, 20 miles north of Chengdu, also acts as a public awareness centre for visitors to teach them about the need to protect bears in Asia and about the available alternatives to bear bile.

VIETNAM
BEAR FARMING

The farming of bears for their bile also takes place in Vietnam, where over 4,000 bears are kept caged in farms around the country. Bile is extracted by tranquilising the bears and draining bile from the gall bladder using syringes. The Vietnamese government acknowledges that bear farming in their country is illegal and should be phased out and is now working with wildlife organisations to register all bears and monitor the bear farms.

In 2008 the Animals Asia Foundation built a bear sanctuary near Hanoi in northern Vietnam which will care for around 200 bears rescued from illegal trade and from farms which close down. Two sanctuary enclosures had been created by late 2010, one for Asiatic black bears and the other for sun bears as both species are found in the wild in and around Vietnam and both have been used in the bear farm industry there.

Local wildlife organisations such as the Education for Nature Vietnam (ENV) and Wildlife at Risk (WAR) are also working to create public awareness about the illegality of bear farming and the need to use alternatives to bear bile.

CAMBODIA
BEAR TRADE

The trade in wildlife in Asia accounts for huge numbers of animals being caught from the wild and traded for use as pets or products. Asiatic black bears are caught from the wild in the forests of Cambodia and sold as pets or for their claws, skin and meat. The methods used to trap the animals often leaves them with serious injuries and rescued bears have frequently been found with missing paws as a result of the leg snares and traps used. The Cambodian Forestry Administration has been working with the Free the Bears Fund since 1997 to rescue bears from this illegal trade. Free the Bears Fund has financed a bear sanctuary near the city of Phnom Penh where

90 rescued bears now live in forested enclosures with water pools and dens.

The bear sanctuary also has a public awareness centre and a mobile education unit which provides a unique opportunity to create awareness of the plight of bears and other wildlife in Cambodia.

BULGARIA
DANCING BEARS

Dancing bears were a common sight in the tourist resorts of Bulgaria up until 2007 when the last dancing bear was legally confiscated.

The use of dancing bears had a long history in Bulgaria, where the local gypsies had traditionally used captive brown bears in the streets of towns and villages to entertain the public. With the modernisation of Bulgaria, in 1990, the sight of a gypsy dragging a ragged bear on a chain through the streets was considered outdated. The gypsies then began using their bears in tourist areas and at beach resorts, obtaining money from tourists for a snapshot of the bear. The bears were kept chained up in the gypsies' gardens when not being dragged around the tourist hot-spots.

In the late 1990s the Bulgarian government agreed to work with animal protection groups to eradicate the cruel use of bears, and a bear sanctuary was constructed at Belitza, 170 km south of the city of Sophia in Bulgaria in 2000. The Austrian animal protection group, Vier Pfoten, funded the project along with the Brigitte Bardot Foundation and helped the authorities rescue over 20 dancing bears from the streets. The last dancing bear was confiscated in 2007 and the practice has now been eradicated. Around 30 brown bears are now cared for at the Bulgarian bear sanctuary which also has a public awareness centre for visitors.

GERMANY
CAPTIVE BEARS

The Austrian based animal protection organisation, Vier Pfoten, built a 1 hectare forest enclosure in Austria in 1998 for 7 rescued brown bears, and built a 3 hectare forest sanctuary in Mueritz, Germany in 2006 which holds 10 brown bears rescued from circuses and poor zoos.

In 1997 a German animal protection group called Foundation for Bears (Stiftung für Bären) created a bear sanctuary and awareness centre in the town of Worbis in the former East Germany. The 'Alternative Bear Park' in Worbis is based in an old unused zoo which has been opened up to create three large natural enclosures measuring several hectares in size.

The Worbis bear sanctuary has rescued 14 bears from circuses and zoos. A pack of rescued wolves also live in the enclosures with the bears. The running costs are covered by the revenue from over 100,000 visitors per year to the bear park which also has a wildlife awareness centre.

BEAR SANCTUARIES AROUND THE WORLD

WSPA
www.wspa-international.org

Greece – Arcturos bear sanctuary
www.arcturos.gr

Hungary
http://medveotthon.hu

India – Wildlife SOS
www.wildlifesos.org/rescue

Pakistan – Bio-resource Research Centre
www.pbrc.edu.pk/

China & Vietnam – Animals Asia Foundation
www.animalsasia.org

Vietnam – Education for Nature Vietnam
www.envietnam.org/our-work/end-bear-crime.html

Cambodia – Free the Bears Fund
www.freethebears.org.au

Bulgaria & Germany – Vier Pfoten
www.vier-pfoten.net/bear-projects.org/

Germany – Worbis bear sanctuary
www.baer.de/abw/index.php

USA – Idaho Black Bear Rehabilitation Centre
www.bearrehab.org/

To find out more information about bear sanctuaries around the world, visit **www.bearsanctuary.com**

Acknowledgements

With thanks to Cristina and Roger Lapis and all the staff of the Libearty Bear Sanctuary in Zarnesti for their unshakable dedication to the rescue and care of bears in Romania, and to the WSPA for the enormous support they have given the Romanian bear sanctuary to help them achieve their aims.

Grateful thanks also to the municipality of Zarnesti who have provided the forest land needed to create the sanctuary and to the Romanian government for undertaking the legal confiscation of captive bears.

Special thanks to my wife for her patience and help with proofreading and grateful thanks to the staff at Pentacor who have expertly guided me through the minefield of publishing.